OREGON MAIN STREET

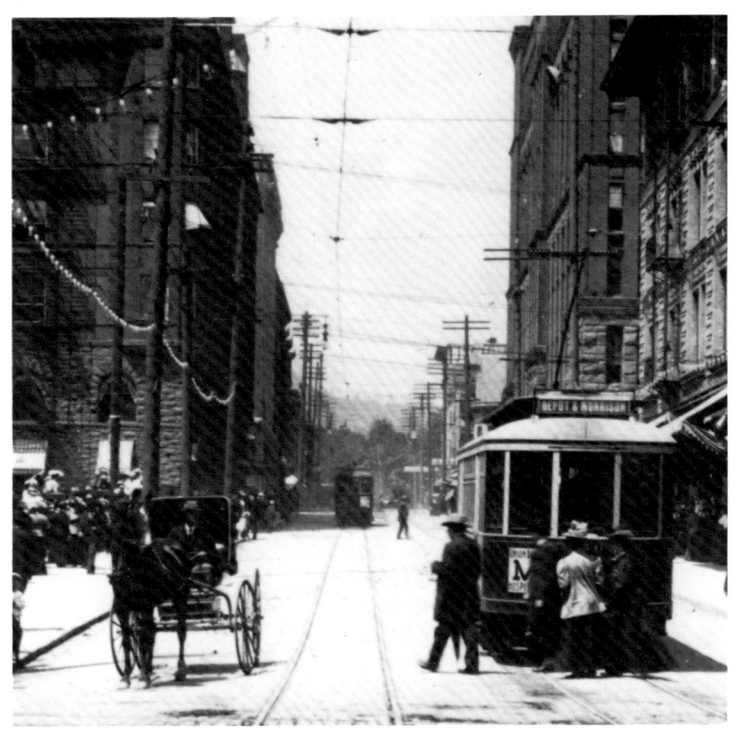

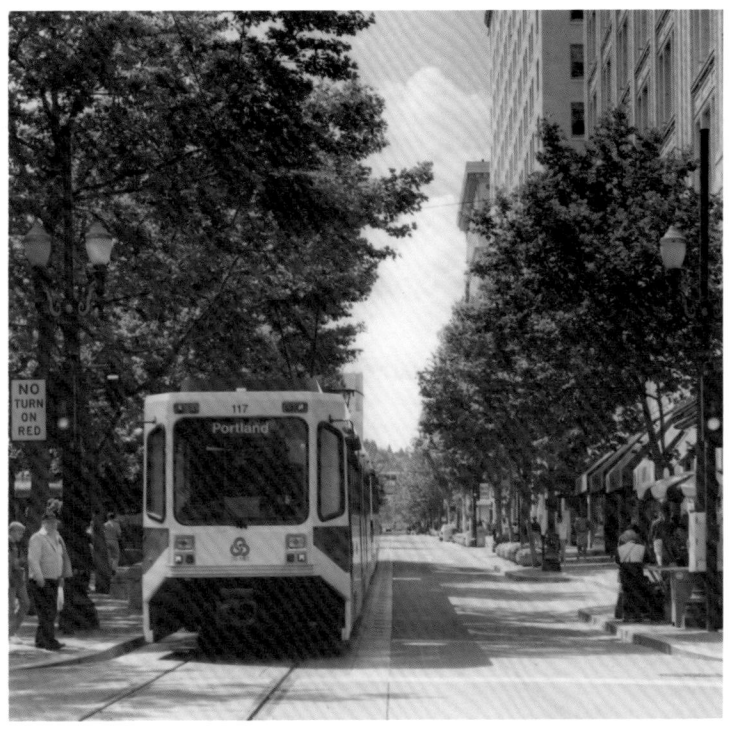

OREGON MAIN STREET

A Rephotographic Survey

James Norman

with text by
Rosiland Clark Keeney
George Kramer
Dwight A. Smith
Dr. Ward Tonsfeldt

Foreword by Susan Seyl

Oregon Historical Society Press

Cover and Title Page Illustrations
Details from Morrison Street, Looking west from SW 5th,
Portland, ca. 1900 and 1994 (OHS Negatives OrHi 9937 and Lot #824-44).

Oregon Historical Society Press
Copyright © 1994, Oregon Historical Society Press.

The paper used in this publication meets the minimum requirements of American National
Standard for Information Sciences--Permanence of Paper for Printed Library Materials,
ANSI Z39.48-1984.

Library of Congress Cataloging-in-Publication Data

Norman, James B., Jr.
   Oregon Main Street: a rephotographic survey / James Norman : with
text by Rosiland Clark Keeney ... [et al.].
      p. cm.
   Includes bibliographic references.
   ISBN: 0-87595-255-0 (Hardcover) – ISBN: 0-87595-256-9 (Softcover)
   1. Streets--Oregon--Pictorial works. 2. Cities and towns--Oregon--History--Pictorial works.
   3. Cities and towns--Oregon--History. 4. Oregon--Pictorial works. I. Keeney, Rosiland Clark,
   1945- . II. Title.
   F877.N67 1994   94-40324
   979.5'009732--dc20   CIP

Printed in the United States of America.

CONTENTS

ACKNOWLEDGEMENTS

A project such as *Oregon Main Street* requires much support and assistance, and the efforts of a number of people and organizations should be recognized. I am particularly indebted to the professional staff at the Oregon Historical Society. Susan Seyl, photographs librarian, coordinated the selection and preparation of the historic images reproduced here and wrote the Foreword to this volume. Evan Schneider, OHS chief photographer, did an exceptional job of printing both the historic and contemporary photographs for the publication and for the attendant exhibition. Dorothy Harrington, exhibits coordinator, provided much initial encouragement for the project, and was responsible for development of the travelling exhibition. Adair Law, managing editor, edited much of the text and coordinated the publication of the book. Bruce Hamilton, Mikki Tint, and Virginia Linnman also deserve thanks for their help and support.

The research staff at the Oregon State Library, including Alden Moberg, Marjorie Napper, Stana Smith, Clair LaBarr, and Judy Leifheit, provided invaluable assistance. Additionally, I wish to acknowledge the research assistance of Stephen Dow Beckham of Lewis and Clark College, Terry Toedtemeier, curator of photography for the Portland Art Museum, and Julie Reese of the Umatilla County Historical Society.

Loretta Harrison, executive director of the Lincoln County Historical Society, Greta Brunschwyler of the Southern Oregon Historical Society, Daniel C. Robertson with the Douglas County Historical Society, Caroline R. Sherrieb with the Oregon Trail Regional Museum, Karen Broenneke, Clatsop County Historical Society, and Dr. Jeffrey Ostler, assistant professor of history at the University of Oregon, through their kind support, were instrumental in the development of the project.

Eric DeLony and Jet Lowe of the Historic American Engineering Record, Eric Eisemann, Cathy Galbraith, Mike Byrnes, Lewis McArthur, Pieter Dykman, Maxine Banks, and Linda Dodds all deserve many thanks for their encouragement and support. I also wish to express my appreciation to Brian Wood, Allan Wood, and the professional staff at Photovision.

Finally, I would like to thank the team of humanities scholars who helped prepare the text for this book. Without the generous efforts of Rosalind Clark Keeney, George Kramer, Dwight Smith, and Ward Tonsfeldt, this project would not have been possible.

FOREWORD

Susan Seyl

An abundance of visual evidence can be found in a main street photograph: architectural styles, the size and configuration of buildings, materials of construction, density of development, modes of transportation, types of businesses, services and social organizations represented and glimpses of street life. Altogether, these factors provide a wealth of information about the town, as well as giving us a sense of the town's character and the role of its main street.

The existence and access to historic photographs of the main streets documented within has made this book possible. The selected historic images, dating from the late nineteenth century through the 1930s, are from the photographic archives of the Oregon Historical Society. Thanks to the efforts of donors, curators and librarians, these visual documents have been saved, cared for and made accessible to the public.

The photographers who created these images were, for the most part, commercial photographers, driven by economics. Wesley Andrews, whose photographs account for nearly half of the selections, was known throughout the Pacific Northwest for his photographic recording of towns. Based in Baker, Oregon, and in Portland after 1929, Andrews traveled throughout Oregon, Washington and Idaho from 1904-1940, making a series of view postcards of each town. Each series usually included shots of the main street, city hall, courthouse, post office, library, hospital, schools, churches, parks, bridges, hotels, residential and business areas, and any other public buildings or notable attractions.

The immense popularity of photographs of town views, particularly picture postcards, created a demand for such images. The majority of Oregon towns, large and small, were experiencing marked growth during the early decades of the twentieth century. Promotional energy and civic pride accompanied this growth and fueled the market for Main Street photographs.

While duplicating the location of the historic views, the contemporary photographs included in this volume were made for an entirely different purpose. The photographer's aim was to examine change over time by matching historic and contemporary views of main streets. This methodology

---

Susan Seyl is the Photographs Librarian for the Oregon Historical Society.

of using visual comparison enhances other types of documentation such as mapping, and will serve future attempts to document and evaluate change.

While a single photograph provides the viewer with a depiction of a place at a particular time, the pairing of contemporary and historic images of the main street of a particular town allows the viewer to compare and interpret. Change, or lack of change, quickly becomes apparent in a way that written descriptions cannot convey. As a body of work, the pairings provide abundant evidence on several fronts, such as patterns of development, and the vital importance of a small town's main street as compared to a city's main street that is just part of a large commercial district.

These pairings invite much more than visual comparisons and academic interpretation, however. The viewer uses this information to pass judgment on these main streets. Was it better then, or is it better now? What aspects of the old and new do we find amazing, beautiful, enlightened, ugly, tragic, surprising, crass, nostalgic, or humorous? Each viewer will have his or her own conclusions about the past versus the present, or perhaps see a continuum that combines elements of the past with the evolving present. It is my hope that these images will serve as powerful statements about Oregon's towns and cities that will inform, entertain, and motivate.

INTRODUCTION

James Norman

Two hundred years ago, the Pacific Northwest region of the United States was an unmapped and virtually unexplored wilderness. The Native American groups who occupied the area intentionally left few permanent signs of their habitation, and because of this, the Lewis and Clark Expedition of 1805 marked a major transition in man's tenure upon the land now called Oregon. Word of this "paradise in the west" quickly reached the eastern part of the country and settlers migrated here to claim their destinies. Carrying with them the customs and patterns of their previous cultures, they established fixed locales for trade and commerce, and the first of Oregon's cities began to rise from the dreams, hopes, and hard work of these brave pioneers. Vestiges of this early urban landscape remain today, tantalizing those who have the patience to observe the signs, symbols and stories of the world of our forebears.

Over the past twenty-five years, considerable interest has developed in the historic and cultural heritage of the United States. Oregon has a particularly rich and colorful story to tell, remarkable due to the short period of time in which it has evolved from wilderness to its current state. As Oregon passes its sesquicentennial anniversary, and many of the state's cities celebrate their one-hundredth anniversaries, there is a heightened interest in local history. The focal point of this interest is on the evolution of community settlements as they developed into the small towns and major cities of the state, and how the growth patterns of Oregon's early settlements have played a defining role in the character of today's urban landscape. This development is embodied in the buildings, transportation facilities, and pedestrian features which line the main streets of our cities. *Oregon Main Street: A Rephotographic Survey* is intended to document the growth and transformation of our urban environment over the past century, to investigate the cultural aspects of the changes which have occurred, and to establish a context in which to evaluate possible directions for future development.

The Rephotographic Survey

The rephotography of historic images provides a powerful tool which can uniquely document and illustrate the effects of time. Like the lines which mark a human face after a lifetime of experience, the facades of our Main Street buildings reflect time's passage. Each period of local economic growth or depression is mirrored by some relic or edifice bearing the features of the popular styles of the day. By focusing on the changes evident along the main streets of Oregon's major cities and small towns, the power and meaning of our cultural evolution become more apparent.

To establish an appropriate context for urban development in Oregon, a group of historic photographs was selected from the archives of the Oregon Historical Society which depict early main street views from a range of time periods and representing large and small cities from all areas of the state. Each of the historic views was then duplicated with a contemporary photograph taken from as near the original location as existing site conditions would allow. The matching historic and contemporary images are presented together to allow a "then vs. now" comparative analysis.

Inherent in the survey is a recognition that Main Street is more than just the buildings which line a thoroughfare, and an assumption that development along Main Street, Oregon, from the past to the present, demonstrates the changes in human endeavors through time: the progression of architectural styles, types of businesses, modes of transportation, the evolution of street design and pedestrian facilities, and even the vagaries of clothing and fashion. To address these issues, and to facilitate a meaningful analysis of the changes, professional humanities scholars specializing in the fields of architectural and cultural history have prepared an essay on the development of Oregon's cities, background information for the three broad regions of the state, and narratives which accompany each of the photographic pairs describing the differences between the historic and contemporary views.

While the narrative descriptions discuss the effects of population, economics, architectural technology, access to transportation, and aesthetic perceptions on the main street environment, the matched pairs of historic and contemporary photographs address these issues graphically and directly. As the viewer assimilates and assesses the many levels of difference between the views, the effect of time on our towns and cities becomes a conscious personal experience.

The examination of matched pairs of historic and contemporary photographs is a visually compelling process which complements and supports the documentary value of rephotography. The concept of rephotography, however, is nearly as old as photography itself, and examples of reproducing images to evaluate the effects of time or change are found in virtually all of photography's primary subject areas. Portraiture, where the growth of one's children is recorded as the years pass; landscape photography, which might compare a particular scene in the blush of spring growth to its appearance during the barren starkness of winter snows; documentary photography, which can examine the progress of construction of a new building or map the growth and alteration of the social environment; even scientific photography, which is used to trace changes over time in the evaluation of chemical reactions, geologic activities, or the nearly imperceptible motion of nearby stars - all fall into the category of rephotography. The ongoing process of satellite image mapping of our planet's surface uses rephotography to detail the effects of all types of changes, from land usage patterns and the growth of population centers, to the tracking of weather system movements and large-scale cataclysms such as the explosion of Mount St. Helens in southern Washington.

The recent publication of comprehensive rephotographic projects, such as *Second View: The Rephotographic Survey Project,* a major NEA-sponsored effort which reproduced the 1870s U.S. Geological Survey expedition photography of Timothy O'Sullivan, William Henry Jackson and others, along with *Frozen Time: A Rephotographic Survey of Lake Tahoe* and *Arizona: Then and Now,* has emphasized the value of this type of work in the understanding of cultural evolution. These projects have established a new protocol for documentation which offers future scholars and researchers a consistent methodology through which cultural development can be analyzed and evaluated.

The Historic Images

The technique of photography, first announced to an astonished public by Louis J. M. Daguerre in 1839, quickly spread throughout the world. By 1840, pioneering photographers had already secured images of major natural and man-made landmarks from all corners of the globe, and as early as 1841, most American cities of any size had daguerreotype studios. it is some indication of the physical and cultural isolation of the Pacific Northwest that it was not until 1851 that daguerreotype operators began arriving in the Oregon Territory. However, within a few short years they established their place among the successful businesses which lined the main streets of Oregon's fledgling towns.

These early photographers recorded the faces of settlers and their families, the majesty of the surrounding natural landscape, and the development which occurred in the rapidly growing urban and trade centers of the new territory. Fortunately, many of the images captured by these, and later photographers, are now preserved in the invaluable collections of the Oregon Historical Society. The record which they provide to researchers, scholars, and even the general viewer is one which could not have been equaled by any amount of journalistic portrayal, or by any other descriptive medium. The expressions on the faces of Oregon pioneers which appear in these early photographs tell of their experiences in a manner even more direct than the stoic words of their diaries. Images of Native Americans offer an abundance of information about the traditions and philosophy of a lifestyle which was rapidly disappearing by the late 1800s. The historic views of our early settlements offer a document which forms the basis for understanding the origins of our contemporary culture.

Historic photographs can have a powerful effect upon a viewer. Almost without exception, these images were executed in a direct, clean style of delineation, and speak of a dignity and grace which rarely appear in contemporary photographic endeavors. The force and energy emanating from certain early photographs can elicit strong personal empathies and stimulate the desire to learn more about the foundations of our lives and customs. Indeed, the rich tonality found in an albumen print from the late 1800s can evoke an intimate feeling of history which echoes in our minds and our memories.

The sheer effort involved in the creation of a large plate photograph a hundred years ago was staggering, and the reasons why certain images were made are often obscure. Unwieldy equipment, fragile glass plates, and a variety of other operational and logistic difficulties required a determination which deterred all but the hardiest of souls. Even well into the twentieth century, to capture a high quality photographic image required a large tripod-mounted sheet-film camera. Yet, in the face of these formidable obstacles, these early photographers worked with a dedication to their craft, convinced of the value of their efforts.

Understanding these difficult conditions, we might wonder why these early photographers would take the time to record a view of the businesses along the main street of their towns. These types of photographs are not often considered artistically or emotionally appealing. In *Amateurs, Photography, and the Mid-Victorian Imagination*, Grace Seiberling indicates that typical photographers of the period, like most modern photographers, "chose not to (document) new buildings or railways, but would travel far to make pictures of an old waterwheel or an ancient dying tree." The commercial value of a main street view for advertisements and postcards would certainly have been a factor, but perhaps there was another, more basic principle also operating here. The innocence of the straightforward compositional themes embodied in these early main street photographs belies the visual strength and temporal resonance which they express. It is hard not to believe that these images were the reflection of a fledgling civic pride; a message to posterity revealing the dreams of these early photographers, and an expression of hope for the future of these new wood frame and brick structures which housed the feedstores, banks, and saloons of our early towns.

The Visual Comparison

In today's culture, we are inundated with photographic imagery. Because of this everyday overexposure to vivid advertising, dramatic portraits, and wildly-angled action shots, all carefully contrived and manipulated, it is the rare image indeed which is powerful enough to capture our attention. The study of photography, as a visual medium, emphasizes the need to make a viewer reach beyond the frame of an image into personal experience. This rephotographic survey provides an opportunity to extend our response beyond the individual image, as each historic and contemporary photograph gains strength through the perspective which one provides the other.

There is an unmistakable difference evident in the historic images when compared to the contemporary views. In some instances, development has resulted in the complete transformation of the main street scene - in others, time appears, at first glance, to have stood still. Yet in every case, the changes in the main street landscape, the very foundation of the urban fabric, are profound. As populations have shifted, local economies have undergone radical alteration, and commercial centers have largely relocated to suburban areas, the functional use and appearance of our downtown structures has been forced to adapt and reconfigure to accommodate these changes, or stagnate in place reflecting a frozen moment in time.

Understanding the basic histories of various cities across the state provides a foundation for the assessment of main street development. The era of early development, the principal economic focus of the area, and the location of a town in relation to major transportation routes establish the basic formula for a town's overall scale, potential for growth, and ultimate success or failure. Periods of boom and bust have occurred throughout the state at different times and for different reasons, and are reflected in the buildings which now line our main streets. The movement in the 1950s to cover old ornate Victorian facades with modern materials affected the appearance of main street in virtually every Oregon city. Other modernization needs, such as street widening, traffic signalization, and an abundance of signage, along with attempts to increase pedestrian appeal, such as planting rows of trees, enhancement of sidewalks with brick detailing, and even the "malling" of downtown streets have also had major effects.

At a fundamental level, the buildings erected in a town whose heyday was in the 1880s are very different from a town which peaked in the early 1920s. For example, a town in eastern Oregon may have been founded in the 1840s because of its juxtaposition to the Oregon Trail. As travel along this trail diminished, the economy of the town may have foundered until a rail line finally reached the area in the 1880s. This boost to the local economy would be reflected in population growth and the construction of several new buildings along Main Street. A devastating fire, so common in our early towns, would likely have destroyed the earliest wood-frame commercial structures, resulting in more stringent building codes which required that newer buildings be constructed of brick. Later changes in transportation access or availability of water may have caused the area's economic base to shift from cattle to sheep, or from gold mining to freight center, resulting in the construction of a new era of main street buildings and renovations. This main street today will display a mixture of architectural styles, urban improvements, and pedestrian features which were popular at different times during its developmental history.

In contrast, many areas along the Oregon coast were not easily accessible until the advent of popular automobile travel in the 1910s and 1920s. Several small coastal communities were "discovered" at this time as tourist attractions for the more populated cities of the nearby Willamette Valley, and their main streets reveal a very different emphasis and appearance than their earlier counterparts in other areas of the state.

By standing where the original photographer stood, by examining the scene before us in comparison to the scene previously recorded, we can see the past become the present. But the present, in this context, no longer represents a fixed position; rather, it becomes merely another step on an endless journey into the future. The efforts of the city planners, architects, and urban visionaries, coupled with the effects of ever-changing economic conditions, have significantly altered the visual and civic nature of our cities' main streets. The rows of main street facades which once were the pride of the early residents have been slowly modified over the years to reflect changing attitudes of architecture, modernization, and "progress." There is a lesson to be learned here. The changes along our main streets mark the passage of time and culture, but often at such a slow rate that we do not often maintain the perspective to consider and understand the cumulative effect of the changes. Only over the span of a lifetime do these changes begin to become apparent, and we can start to appreciate what has occurred.

THE DEVELOPMENT OF OREGON'S CITIES

Dwight A. Smith

"The relationships of early encampments and trails, buildings, villages and cities to the surround of natural environment were gradually revealed...in a rich manner, demanding much more evaluation...of the effects of social, economic and political factors in contemporary relationships. Time was when the sink-or-swim-come-what-may attitudes held by strong and clever survivors held their peculiar charm. But now our most desirable spaces have become alarmingly finite - the present at least - and it is imperative that bolstered by what we know, we look into the dark glass of the future. After all social, economic and political factors are man-made...We can still be the masters of our spatial fate."

Thomas Vaughan, Introduction to *Space Style and Structure: Building in Northwest America* (1974).

In a short essay on city building in the Oregon Country, it would be convenient to start in Oregon City in the 1840s. This sesquicentennial-celebrated town was a destination and result of the major migration of Americans to the Pacific Northwest, and substantially began the creation of what is now the state of Oregon.

The cultural heritage of the Oregon Country, however, extends much further back and it would be embarrassingly ethnocentric not to mention preceding events in the continuum of town and city history. The layering of heritage in Oregon began about 11,000 years ago when Clovis-pointed hunters arrived. It is speculative when the aboriginal Indians settled into villages, but evidence along the Oregon coast and Columbia River indicates that large concentrations of native peoples were present for 5,000 years. Their "lost cities" functioned as service and trading centers as do our present ones, and were quite complex. The names of most of these villages are not commonly known, but many still exist in the names of current cities and counties such as Tualatin, Clatskanie, Tillamook, Yachats, Multnomah, Clackamas, and Wasco.

Dwight A. Smith is a Senior Cultural Historian for ODOT, and was the principal author of Historic Highway Bridges of Oregon.

The most important Oregon "city" at the beginning of the Euro-American influence in the Pacific Northwest was not located within the current state boundaries, but its contribution to Oregon's development was significant. Fort Vancouver, north across the Columbia River, was built in 1825 by the Hudson's Bay Company by Chief Factor John McLoughlin (who would later move to Oregon City and become the "Father of Oregon"). The fort complex soon became a major fur trading and supply center, with company ships arriving and departing on the Columbia River. It was a busy, surprisingly cosmopolitan place. In the 1830s, Fort Vancouver had 500 - 700 residents and extensive agriculture lands. The first settlers in Oregon were former Hudson's Bay Company French Canadian trappers from the fort who settled in the French Prairie area (of Marion County) in the late 1820s through the early 1840s. St. Paul, founded in 1838 by Fr. Francis Norbett Blanchet, and Champoeg (1840s) were French-speaking towns in French Prairie.

The push-pull influences in the American east, midwest and south in the mid-1800s resulted in a major migration of overland settlers to the Oregon Country. The land in Oregon's western valleys was fertile and available, the native population was not violent, and, with missionary and patriotic zeal, dreams of a better life brought the overlanders west. What started as a trickle, became a torrent in the 1840s, 1850s and 1860s, as the Oregon Trail, Applegate Trail and Barlow Road gained national significance as routes of history.

Town and city development was part of the dream of Oregon's new residents. Although there is an idealization of the overland immigrant as being agrarian, many wagons were filled with merchants, traders, craftsmen, millwrights and smiths ready to make their destinies in town and city, rather than on the farm. As soon as provisional and territorial government was in place, numerous new town plats were filed with the counties, many of which never saw further activity.

Oregon's first towns were developed along navigable rivers, principally the Columbia and Willamette, and mainly in the Willamette Valley. The rivers served as transportation routes for goods and services and also provided water power for flour and lumber mills. These towns were sited with proximity to fertile agriculture lands and frequently on or near earlier Indian village sites. The settlers created towns and cities in the image of those they had left behind, but juxtaposed onto the Oregon landscape. The pioneer period resulted in the application of a large number of eastern place names to Oregon cities, generally for sentimental reasons (e.g., Portland, Salem and Albany). The towns also were named for their colorful founders (e.g., Eugene City, Roseburg and Brownsville).

The first census in Oregon was taken in 1845, when 2,109 persons were counted. Another census was taken in 1850 by the federal government after

Oregon had become a territory in 1845. This census showed 13,294 residences. The 1850 census included four towns in the Willamette Valley - Oregon City, rival Portland and Linn City (now West Linn) and Multnomah City (no longer existing, below Linn City). In 1853, there were 39 post offices in the Willamette Valley, many serving communities which would take off in growth - Hillsboro (1850), Lafayette (1846), Independence (1852), Dallas (1840s), Corvallis (1840s), Salem (1840), Brownsville (1853), Albany (1848) and Eugene (1852), to name a few.

Oregon City, incorporated in 1857, was the first successful town in Oregon and was the territorial capital during the 1840s and 1850s. Portland, downstream on the Willamette River, however, had better access to farming regions and was at the head of navigation for ocean transport. Portland also had better luck and more aggressive salesmanship. After its founding in the mid-1840s and incorporation in 1857, Portland quickly became Oregon's chief economic metropolis. The first Portland census in 1850 showed 821 residents.

City development quickly spread to southern Oregon after initial settlement in the Willamette Valley, as well as to the Clatsop Plains area of the northwest coast. Roseburg and neighboring Winchester started in the 1850s, as did Ashland in the Bear Creek Valley. Jacksonville, the original county seat of Jackson County, began with the placer gold discoveries there in 1851-52.

The Dalles, east of the Cascades, started with a Methodist mission in 1838, and was an important point on the Oregon Trail and Barlow Road. Umatilla also started early and was incorporated by 1864. Town development in the rest of central and eastern Oregon occurred later than the rest of the state, awaiting the expansion of the cattle and sheep raising industry and logging. The discovery of gold in eastern Oregon in the 1861-62 period created boom and bust communities, but also contributed to the long term establishment of cities, such as Canyon City, Baker City, La Grande, Burns, Prineville and Klamath Falls, most incorporating in the 1880s.

The Oregon coast's fishing and logging towns started small and mostly remained so until after the turn of the century. Scottsburg (1850), Port Orford (1850s), Gardiner (1851) and Empire City (1853), later part of Coos Bay, were the historic beginnings on the coast.

Railroad construction in Oregon had a major impact on city development, bringing a new prosperity to the existing cities on the rail lines and causing stagnation or decline to those bypassed. The Oregon and California Railroad (Southern Pacific), running north and south through the state, began construction in Portland in 1868, finally reaching Ashland in 1887. The next major railroad was the Oregon Railway and Navigation Company (Union Pacific) along the Columbia River completed in 1883, connecting Oregon cities with the transcontinental system. Highway development, particularly the Interstate program of the 1960s and 1970s, tended to border the rail lines and assisted in the economic take-off of Oregon's service centers.

City development is a fascinating chapter in Oregon's history. Today there are 240 incorporated cities. Many more are not incorporated or are no more - ghost towns of the boom and bust periods or victims of flooding and fires. Some never quite recuperated after the county seat was moved elsewhere, or after the charismatic religious leader left or died. A few types of communities, like company logging towns, hang on for at least a few more years. However, even today, new towns are forming, as retirement and recreation stimulate growth in previously unpopulated areas.

But the nature of our cities has changed significantly over the past century. The arrival of the automobile was accompanied by a need to vastly increase and improve the system of roads in Oregon, and opened up newly accessible areas for development. In 1914, there were only twenty-five miles of paved roads in Oregon. By 1930, there were 2,600 miles of hard surface roads and 1,700 miles of gravel roads on the state highway system. The ease and speed of travel has changed the way people live and, consequently, the focus and function of our cities and towns.

The existing infrastructure of our cities and towns was not prepared for the needs of this new and immediately popular form of transportation. Ever-increasing numbers of cars and trucks prompted civic improvements to accommodate the requirements of parking, traffic management and pedestrian safety.

The freedom which the automobile provided severed the intimate connection which a less mobile population had to the central commercial core of our cities. The shifting of major residential areas to the suburbs and the consequent relocation of retail and commercial activities to outlying malls have left many downtown buildings vacant. The result has been a major alteration of both the civic nature and visual appearance of our downtowns. For many years, the older structures along our main streets were considered eyesores and many were destroyed, to be remembered only through the fleeting images captured in historic photographs. It has only been during the past twenty years or so that the revitalization of our downtown areas has begun, in concert with new historic preservation values of our citizenry. Interestingly, the nostalgia and visual appeal of the remaining older buildings have helped stimulated a new feeling of downtown cohesion and an awareness of the significance of these early structures in the larger understanding of Oregon's development.

Oregon started small in population, and expanded with huge migrations in the last century. The state's current population is about 3,000,000, of which two thirds are in metropolitan areas. At the end of this century and into the next, Oregon is expecting major increases in population, including another million in the Portland metropolitan area by the year 2040. The future of our city growth will, no doubt, result in changes which we cannot as yet foresee, and we can but wonder how the main streets of our cities will appear to subsequent generations, if they survive at all. The railroad's early arrival and later highway and interstate development have drastically changed our cities. Only futurists and visionaries can predict the results of the latest transportation change, the computerized information superhighway.

It is perhaps appropriate to close with a passage from Lewis Mumford's *The City in History:*

> "If we would lay a new foundation for urban life, we must understand the historic nature of the city, and distinguish between its original functions, those that have emerged from it, and those that may still be called forth. Without a long running start in history, we shall not have the momentum needed, in our own consciousness, to take a sufficiently bold leap into the future; for a large part of our present plans, not least many that pride themselves on being 'advanced' or 'progressive,' are dreary mechanical caricatures of the urban and regional forms that are now potentially within our grasp.

> The final mission of the city is to further man's conscious participation in the cosmic and the historic process. Through its own complex and enduring structure, the city vastly augments man's ability to interpret these processes and take an active, formative part in them, so that every phase of the drama it stages shall have, to the highest degree possible, the illumination of consciousness, the stamp of purpose, the color of love. That magnification of all the dimensions of life, through emotional communion, rational communication, technological mastery, and above all, dramatic representation, has been the supreme office of the city in history. And it remains the chief reason for the city's continued existence."

NORTHWESTERN OREGON

Rosalind Clark Keeney

Portland	*Corvallis*	*Astoria*
Salem	*Eugene*	*Tillamook*
Albany		*Newport*

The image of the "Garden of Eden" which attracted thousands of pioneers across the Oregon Trail in the 1840s was the Willamette Valley of northwestern Oregon. Descriptions sent east by map makers, missionaries and inland explorers depicted an area offering fertile open land, ample rainfall, a temperate climate, navigable rivers and a good supply of timber. Any other location was just "so much dry, rugged country to be endured in order to reach that goal."

The northwest portion of the Oregon, particularly the Willamette Valley, was settled quickly because of the free land offered by the government. The Dalles and Oregon City were the original destinations of those traveling the Oregon Trail, but other towns were soon established as trading centers along the Willamette River. The north coast was sparsely populated since it was isolated and hard to reach due to the coastal mountain range, and because the sandy soil and wet cool climate was not as good for agricultural production. However, towns were formed in Astoria, Tillamook and Newport due to their natural harbors.

The railways, which were built in the 1870s and 1880s, made it possible for towns in the Willamette Valley to prosper because the crops and lumber produced there could reach larger markets. From the turn of the century until now, the major factor of change has been the automobile. The construction of new transporation routes, and particulary the completion of the Interstate highway system, has allowed explosive growth in the population centers and fertile agricultural lands of the Willamette Valley, and opened up once remote coastal areas for new development.

Rosiland Clark Keeney is a Cultural Historian for ODOT, a Preservation Planner for the City of Albany, and is the author of Architecture, Oregon Style.

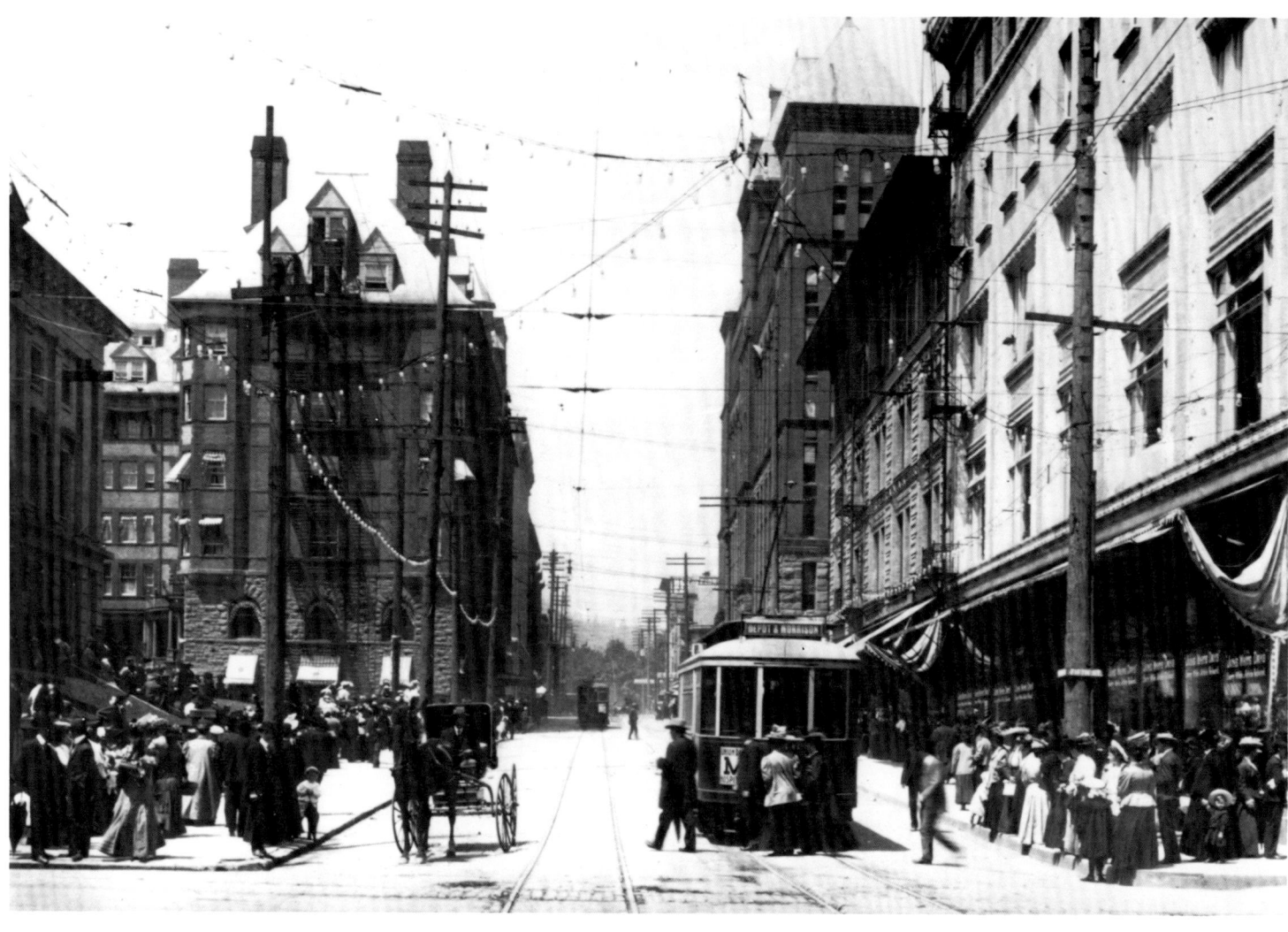

SW Morrison Street, looking west from Fifth, Portland, ca. 1900 (OHS Neg. OrHi 9937)

Portland 1900-1994

Portland was established in 1844 by two new England transplants, Asa Lovejoy, and Francis Pettygrove, who flipped a penny to decide what the town would be named - Boston lost. The town was incorporated in 1851 and gradually became a great wharf city by the 1860s supporting 3,000 souls. Impressive thoroughfares of elegant and massive buildings were erected from First to Sixth Streets by the 1890s. And while Portland was not the most sophisticated city on the west coast, it supported all the elements of an intellectual and civilized society, and its population grew rapidly from 60,000 in 1890 to 207,314 by 1910.

Fires destroyed a total of 30 blocks of the original central city in 1872 and 1873, resulting in a rebuilding boom. The Pioneer Courthouse Office (1873), on the left side of the photograph, escaped the fires because it was built at a site considered to be far out of town at the time. It is now the oldest surviving public building in the Pacific Northwest. The massive Queen Anne building on the left side of the photograph was the seven-story Portland Hotel (1890). With its dormers, towers, and arched openings, this McKim, Mead, and White-designed chateau-like building was the pride of Portland.

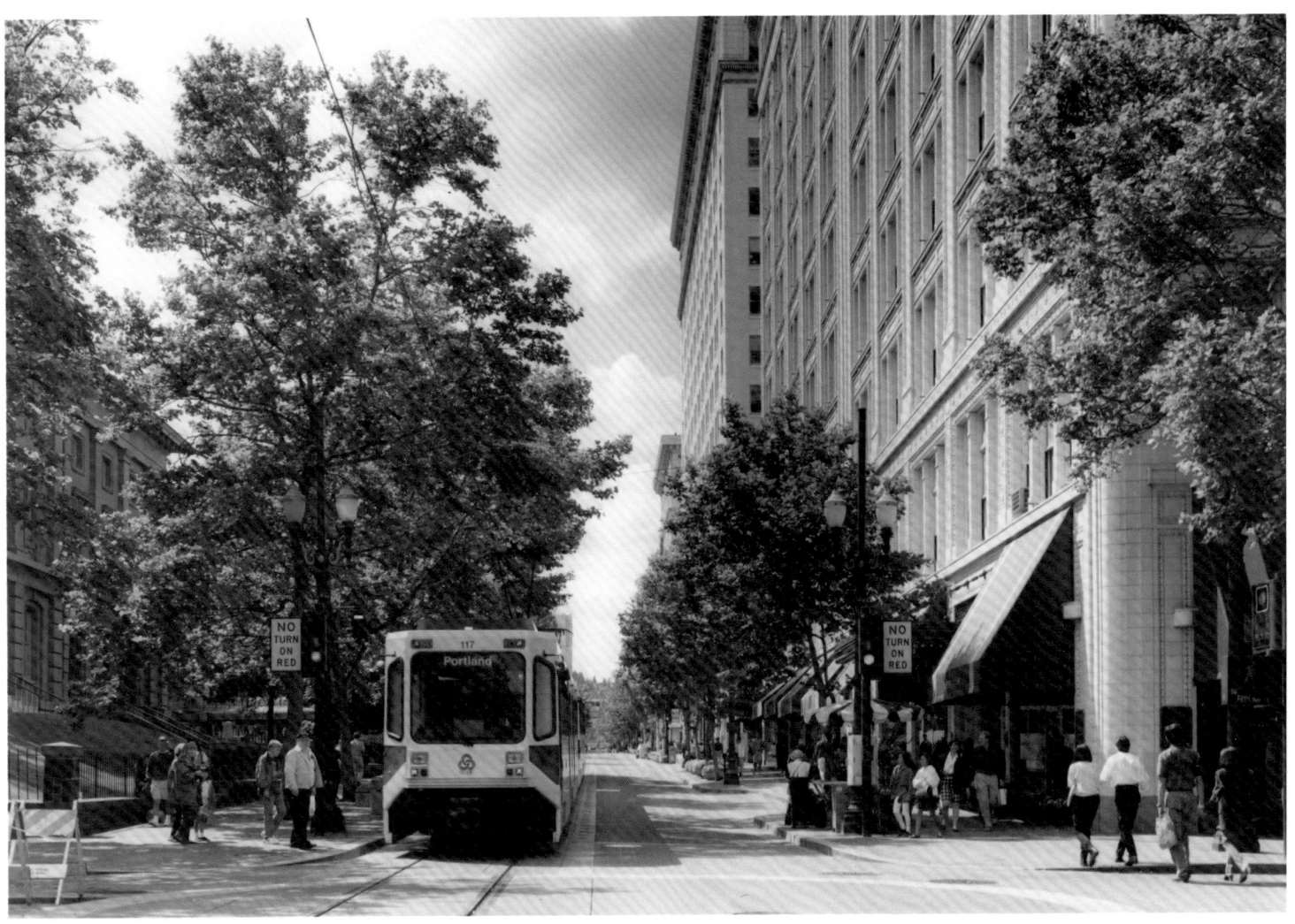

SW Morrison Street, looking west from Fifth, Portland, 1994 (OHS Neg. Lot 824-44)

The Pioneer Courthouse now stands at the center of modern Portland. In 1933, a new federal courthouse was built and the original courthouse seemed doomed for destruction, but in the 1970s it became the seminal rallying point for the preservation movement in Oregon. It was rehabilitated and became the Circuit Court Building. Fate was not so kind to the old Portland Hotel; it was razed in 1951 to become a parking lot. The Meier and Frank Building (1898) on the right side of the historic photograph was replaced in 1915 by a newer Meier and Frank building which featured white glazed terra-cotta. The rather short life of the first building was a direct result of Sigmund Frank's visit to Chicago where he was so impressed by the Carson, Pirie, Scott building (1904), designed by Louis Sullivan, that he decided to modernize and increase the size of his building when he returned to Portland.

Today this area of town is still the heart of Portland. The parking lot was replaced by the Pioneer Courthouse Square in 1983, incorporating the wrought iron gate and fencing from the Portland Hotel. The Tri-Met lightrail system added in 1986 is now the highlight of the city's public transport system.

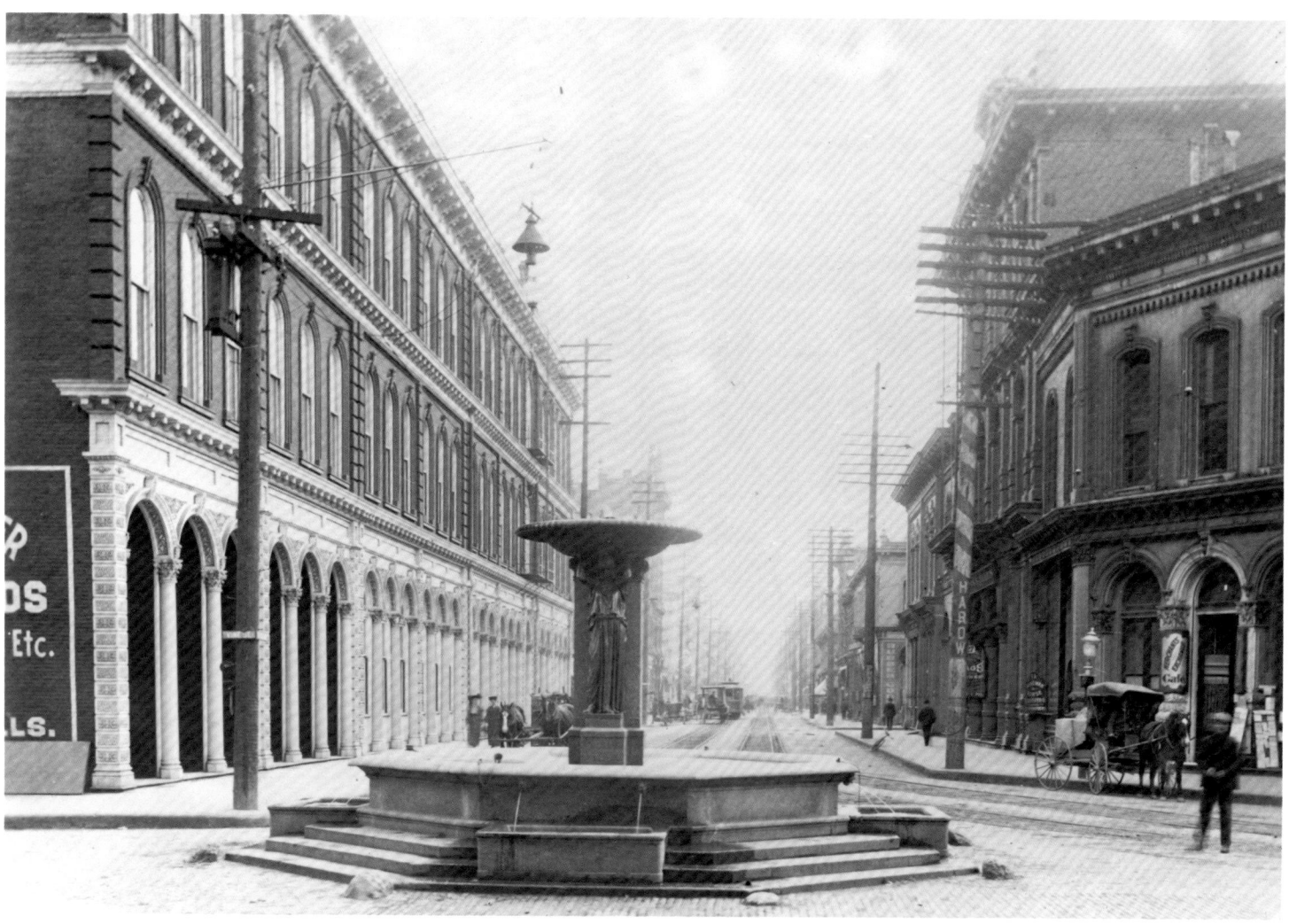

SW First Avenue, looking south from Ash, Portland, ca. 1895 (OHS Neg. OrHi 27417)

Portland 1895-1994

The Skidmore Fountain (1888) stands at the center of these photos. When constructed it was the heart of Portland and was superbly sited so that five streets radiated from its base. Designed by nationally-prominent New York sculptor Olin L. Warner, the octagonal granite structure collects water in its lower troughs from spouting lions heads. It was partially bequeathed by Stephen Skidmore as a convenience of horses, men and dogs. The fountain and the neighborhood fell into bad times as the city moved uptown. Horses no longer needed to be refreshed by fountains when the automobile arrived and the area was no longer the fashionable center of town.

The three-story New Market Theater Building (1872) located on the right side of the photograph had a two-hundred foot long interior arcade lined with produce stalls on the first floor, a 1,200 seat theater on the second floor, and a cafe on the third level. When it was replaced by the Tivoli, a bigger and better theater building, it was

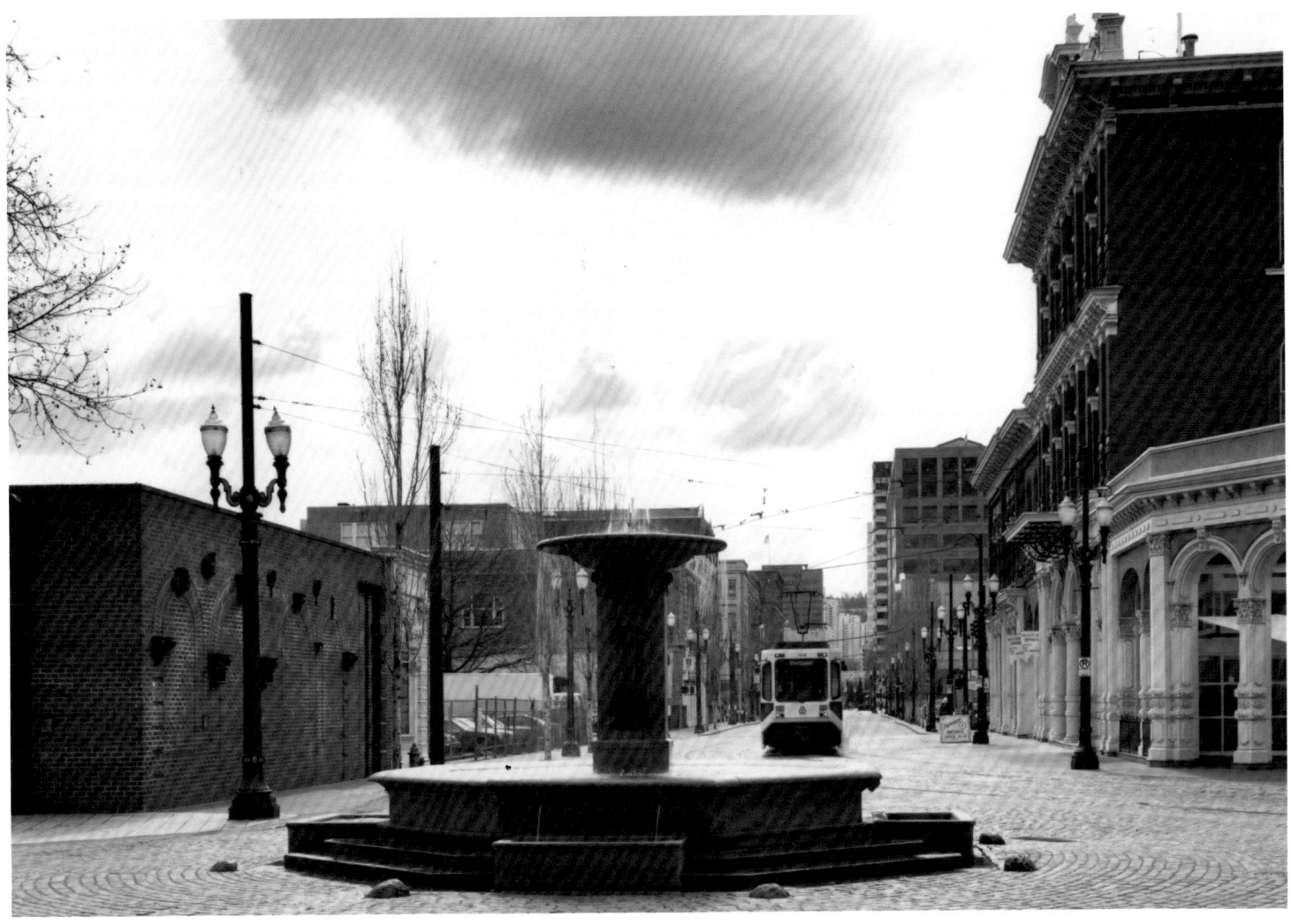

SW First Avenue, looking south from Ash, Portland, 1994 (OHS Neg. Lot 824-2)

eventually relegated to a warehouse and finally a parking garage by the 1970s. The magnificent cast-iron fronted Ankeny and Lewis & Flanders Block (1869) was demolished to make way for the Central Fire Station in the 1940s. The brick wall now on the site was erected in 1981 to separate the area from the fire department.

The area was designated a Historic District by the City of Portland in 1975 and has undergone a renaissance. The New Market Theater Building was restored in 1982-83 and is now a vital commercial center with restaurants and small specialty shops. The corner two-story New Market Block, North Wing (1873) was destroyed in 1956 but its beautiful cast-iron arcade was reconstructed with a fiberglass reproduction in 1984 to enhance the street and serve as a visual reminder of Portland's cast-iron legacy.

Salem 1915-1994

This set of photographs features the Ladd and Bush Bank Building (1869-70, now the U.S. National Bank). The elaborate cast-iron facade of this building is one of Oregon's most extravagant examples. It was designed by John Nestor and produced at the Willamette Iron Works Company in Portland and is patterned after a sixteenth-century library in Venice. It features a corner entry, rusticated pilasters with Corinthian capitals, and five keystones on each arch. In 1967 this building was doubled in size, and a new concrete wall was poured and covered by the cast-iron facade salvaged from the Ladd and Tilton Bank of Portland (1868) when it demolished in 1954. It is now the largest cast-iron-fronted structure on the west coast. On the left is the Dearborn building (1874) which was remodeled in the mid-1920s.

Beyond the Ladd and Bush Bank in the contempoary photograph is the Lively Building (1927), Salem's first skyscraper. The historic view features the electric trolley that was established in 1890 and served until 1926. One of Salem's newer city buses is evident in the modern view. Further down State Street stands one of Salem's most notable landmarks, the steeple of the First United Methodist Church. This church was designed by noted architect Cass Chapman and built in 1877-78 on the site of the first First Methodist Church erected west of the Rockies. Note the man on top of the Ladd and Bush Bank Building in the historic photo installing finials on the roof.

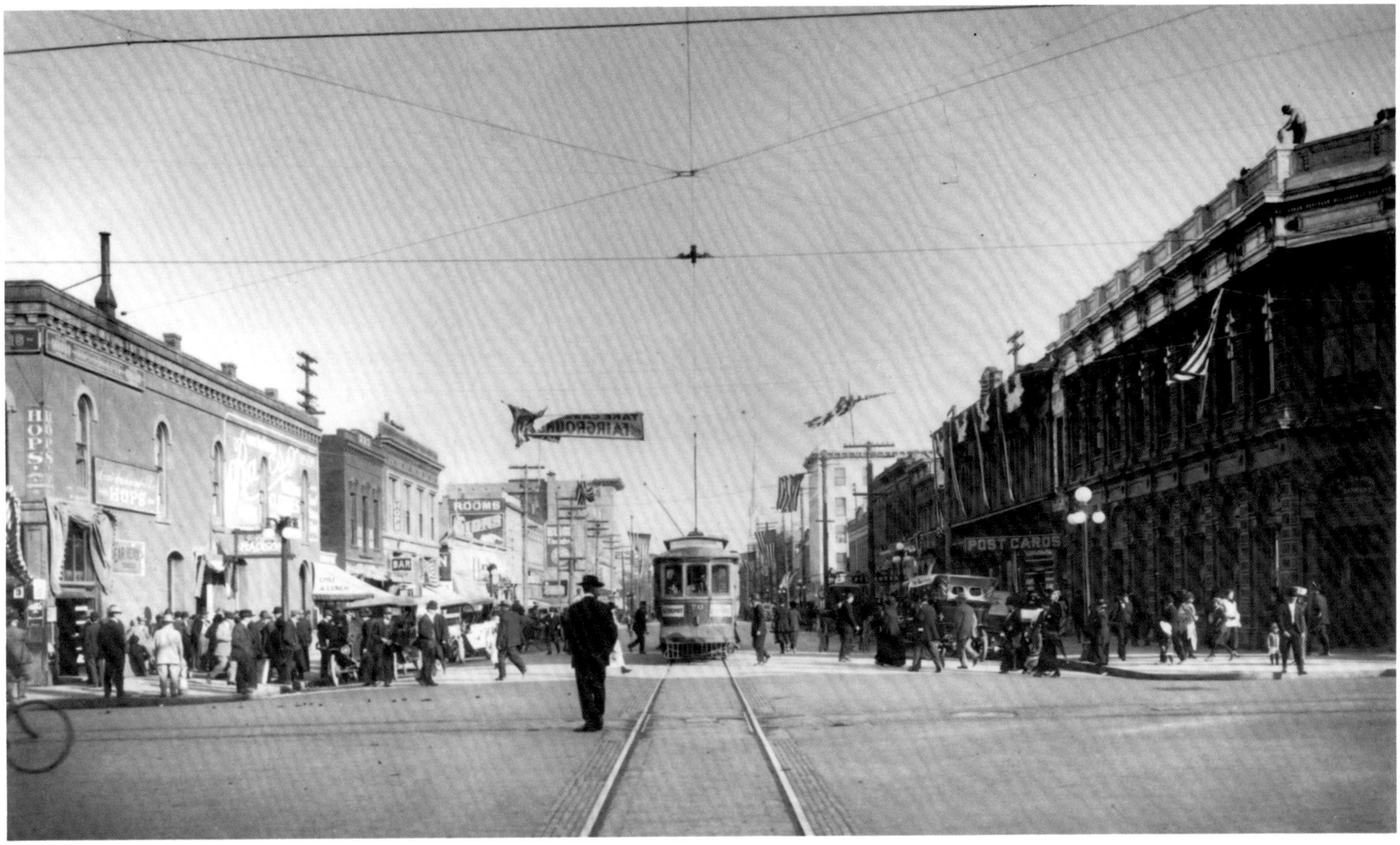

State Street, looking east from Commercial, Salem, ca. 1915 (OHS Neg. OrHi 23083)

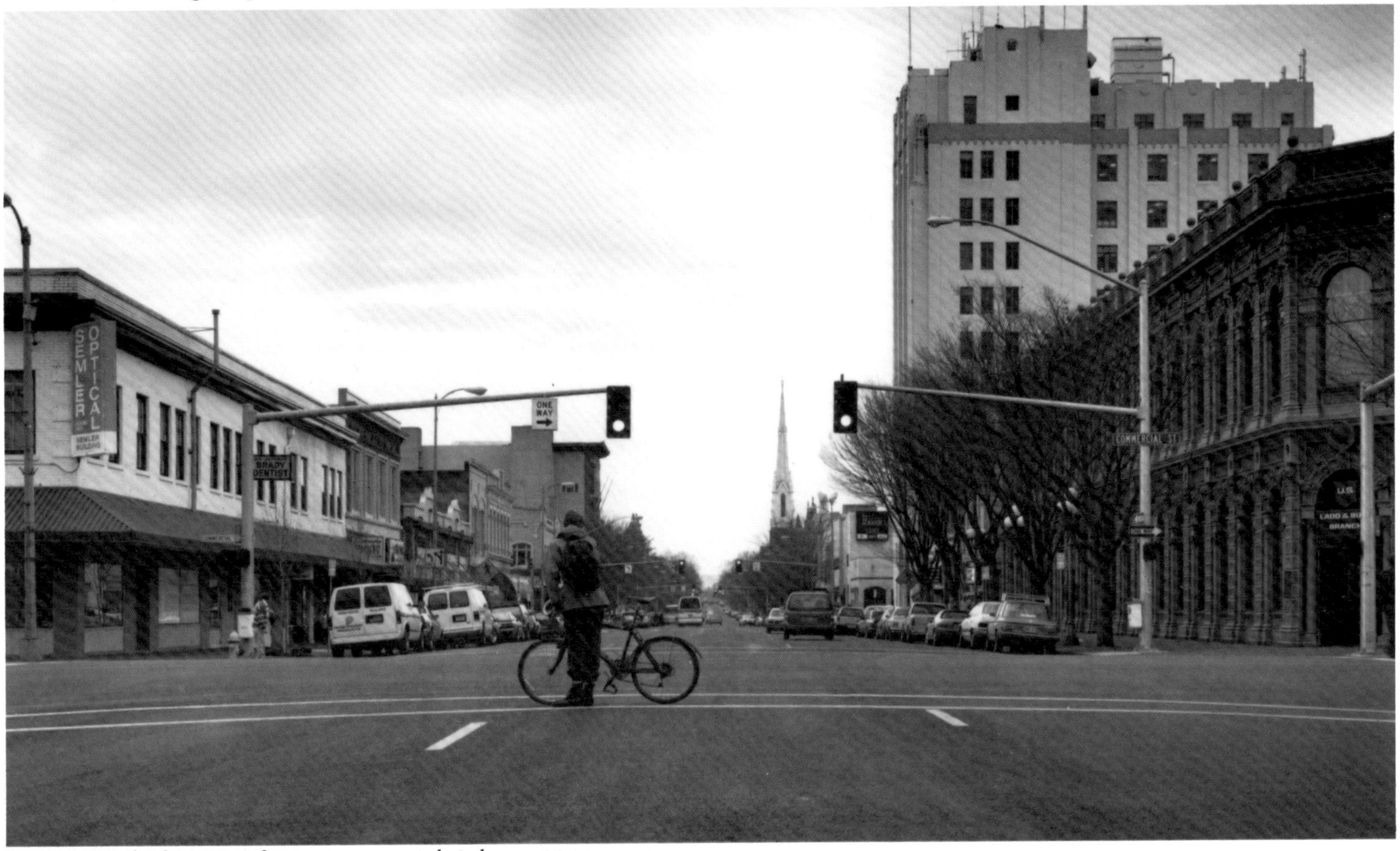

State Street, looking east from Commercial, Salem, 1994 (OHS Neg. Lot 824-3)

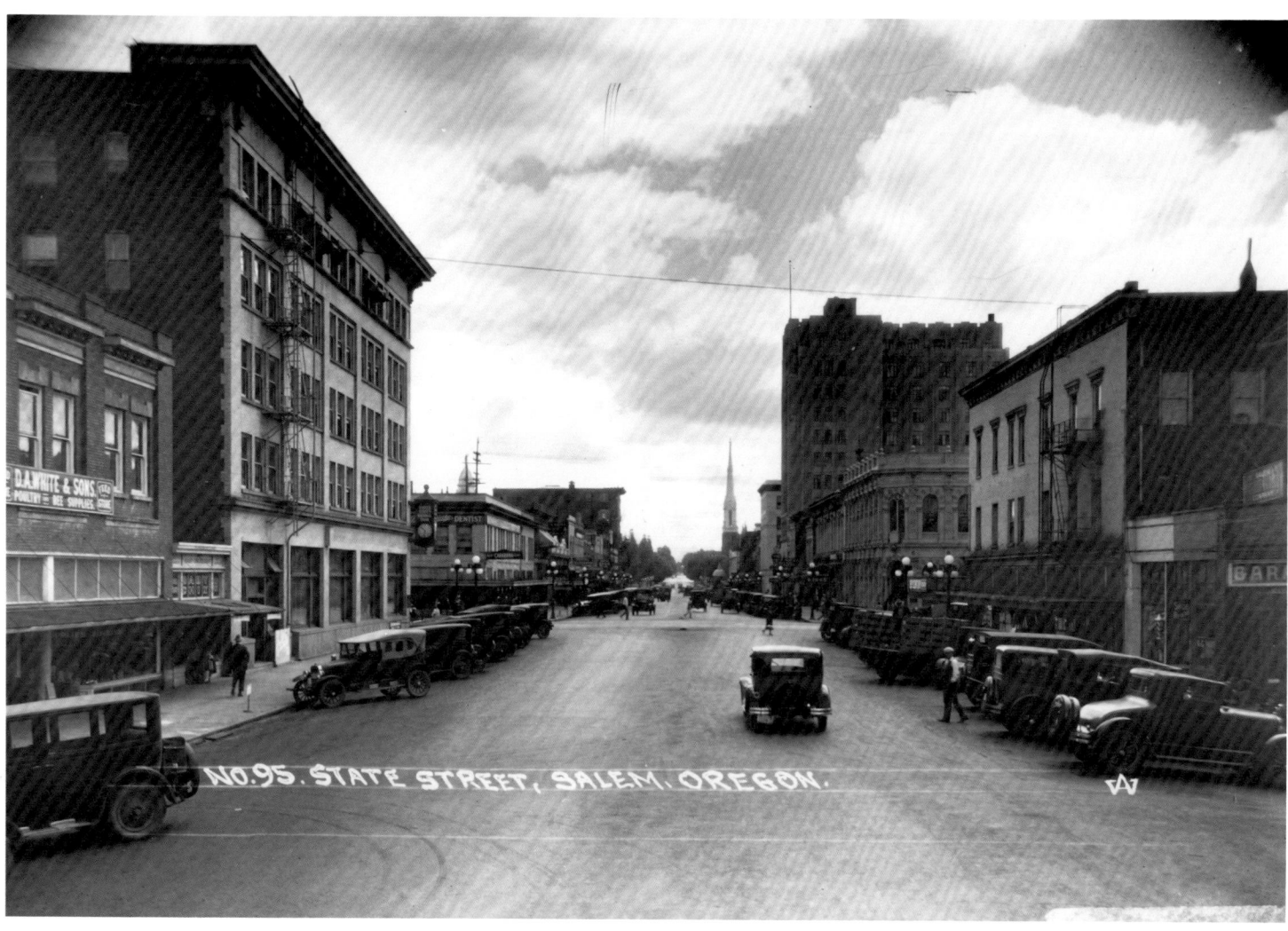

State Street, looking east from Front, Salem, ca. 1930 (OHS Neg. OrHi 18072)

Salem 1930-1994

The name Salem comes from Shalom, a Hebrew word for peace. The area was settled by Methodist missionary Jason Lee in the mid-1840s. He laid out a town and sold off lots to finance the Oregon Institute, the first school for Euro-American children west of the Mississippi and the foundation for Willamette University (1852). In 1851, the town was selected as the territorial capital (although the capital was moved to Corvallis for a short time in 1855) and developed as a riverfront commercial and civic center. The railroad reached Salem from Portland in 1871 and the town's growth accelerated as new industries were established to provide jobs for the growing population.

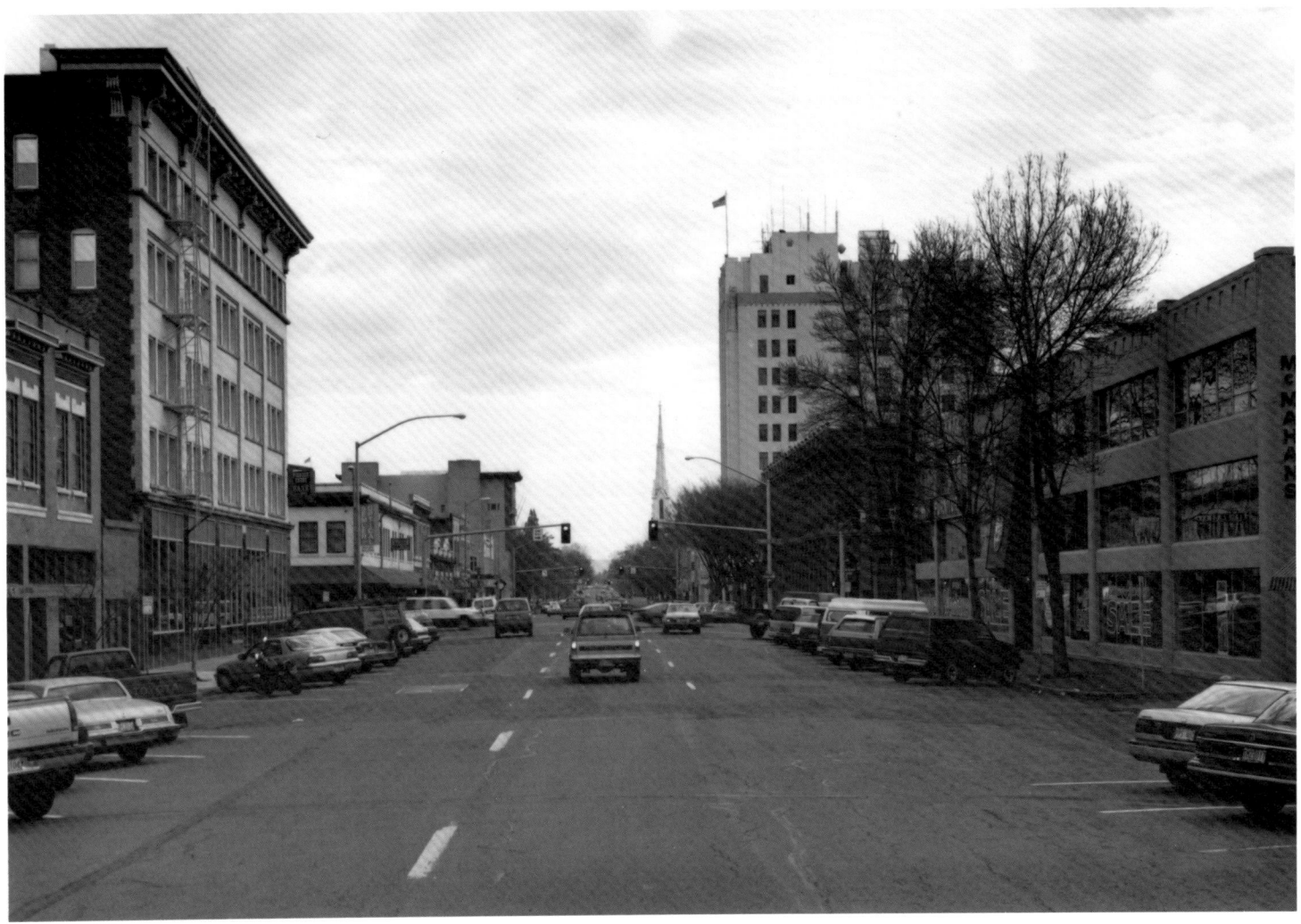

State Street, looking east from Front, Salem, 1994 (OHS Neg. Lot 824-4)

The tall building right of center with the griffins perched at the corners is the Lively Building (1927), Salem's first skyscraper. Beyond it is the spire of the First United Methodist Church (1877-78), another Gothic architecture-inspired building. The U.S. National Bank Building (1909), now called the Pioneer Trust Building, on the left was Salem's first steel and concrete building.

Note State Street's 99-foot width. The grand avenue was laid out in the 1860s in optimistic anticipation that Salem would become the diplomatic and political center of the state.

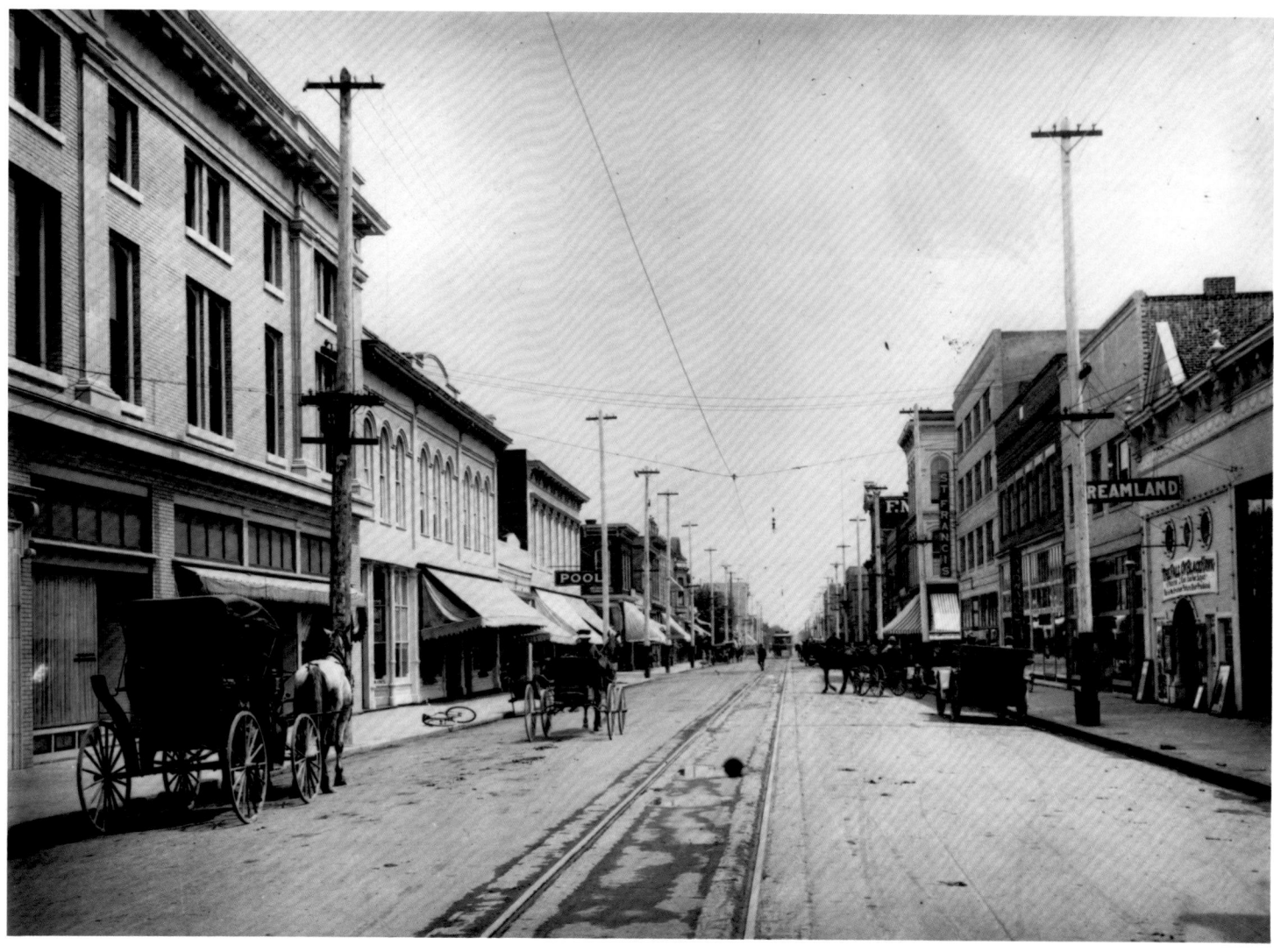

West 1st Street, looking east from Washington, Albany, ca. 1920 (OHS Neg. OrHi 53485)

Albany 1920-1994

Albany was established in 1848 by two brothers from New York who came west intending to found a town. They purchased a claim at the confluence of the Willamette and Calapooia Rivers for $400 and a Cayuse pony from a man who was ready to move on, and laid out town lots. Designated the county seat in 1851, the town grew and in 1852 the first steamboat arrived. Commercial buildings were built along First and Second Avenues and the busy river port city became the hub of the mid-valley and grew rapidly. In 1871, the railroad arrived and was celebrated as the greatest event in Albany's history.

In 1909, the town was electrified, and one year later the streets were paved and concrete sidewalks added to the downtown. Another railway came to Albany (Oregon Electric) and by 1912, twenty-eight trains were operating daily going in five different directions. More multimodal than today's automobile society, people went from place to place by horses, bikes, automobile, and the electric street car. The building on the left is the Masonic Hall, built in 1880 and modernized in 1915. The

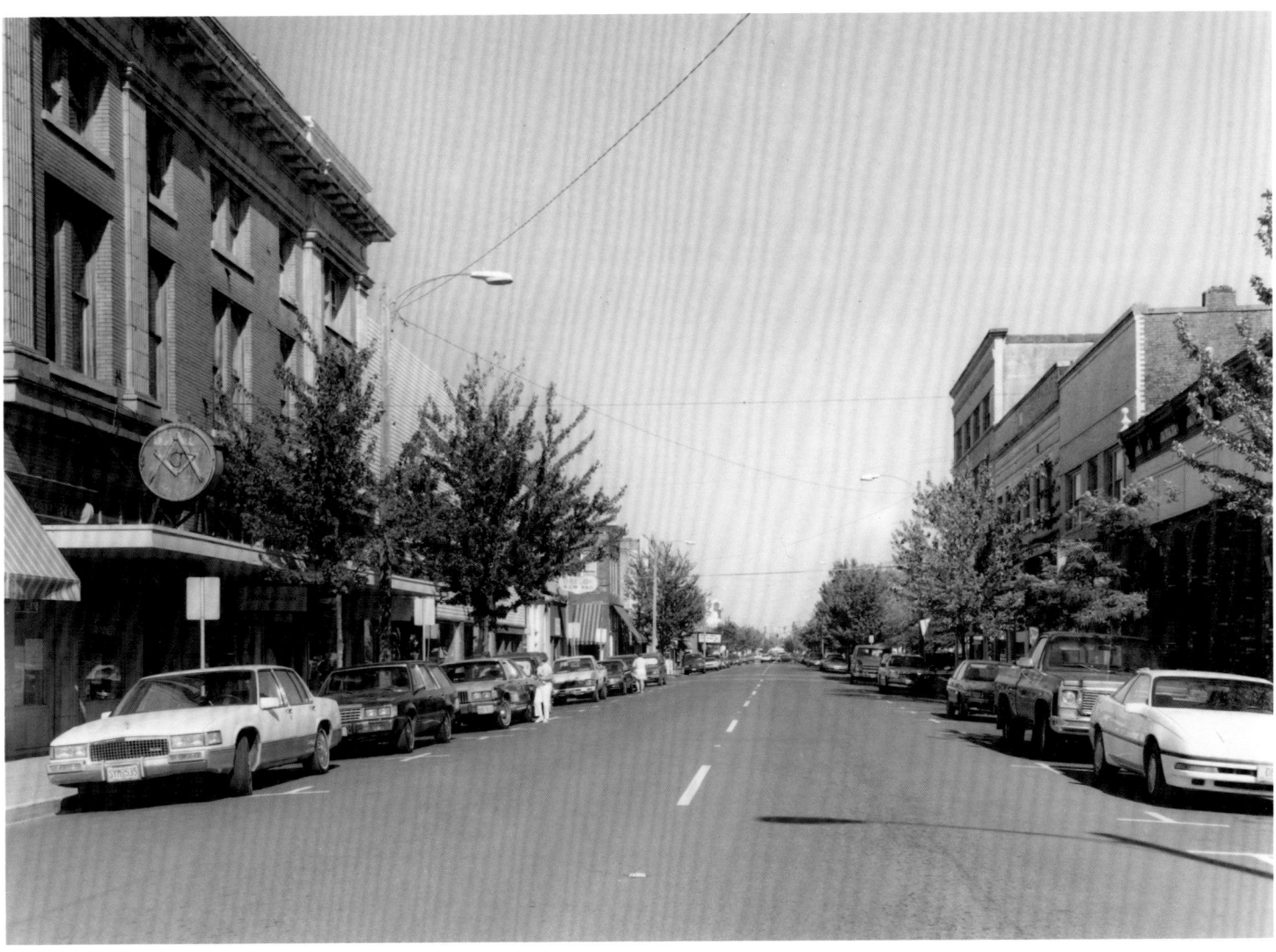

West 1st Street, looking east from Washington, Albany, 1994 (OHS Neg. Lot 824-45)

Dreamland Theater Building (the location of the first general store) on the right was a penny arcade where the more adventurous paid a cent to see exotic photographs and play games. The four-story St. Frances Hotel (1912) was and continues to be the tallest building in the downtown.

Most historic commercial buildings in Albany remain remarkably intact today and were designated a historic district on the National Register of Historic Places in 1982. Albany also became a National Trust Main Street town that year. Since that time, the old commercial center has had an economic, and spiritual revival, embodying the spirit of the National Trust Main Street program. The historic district now boasts a growing number of antique and specialty stores that attract visitors and shoppers from all over Oregon. A recent development is the arrival of urban homesteaders who are moving into and refurbishing the second stories of the commercial buildings and converting them into comfortable apartments.

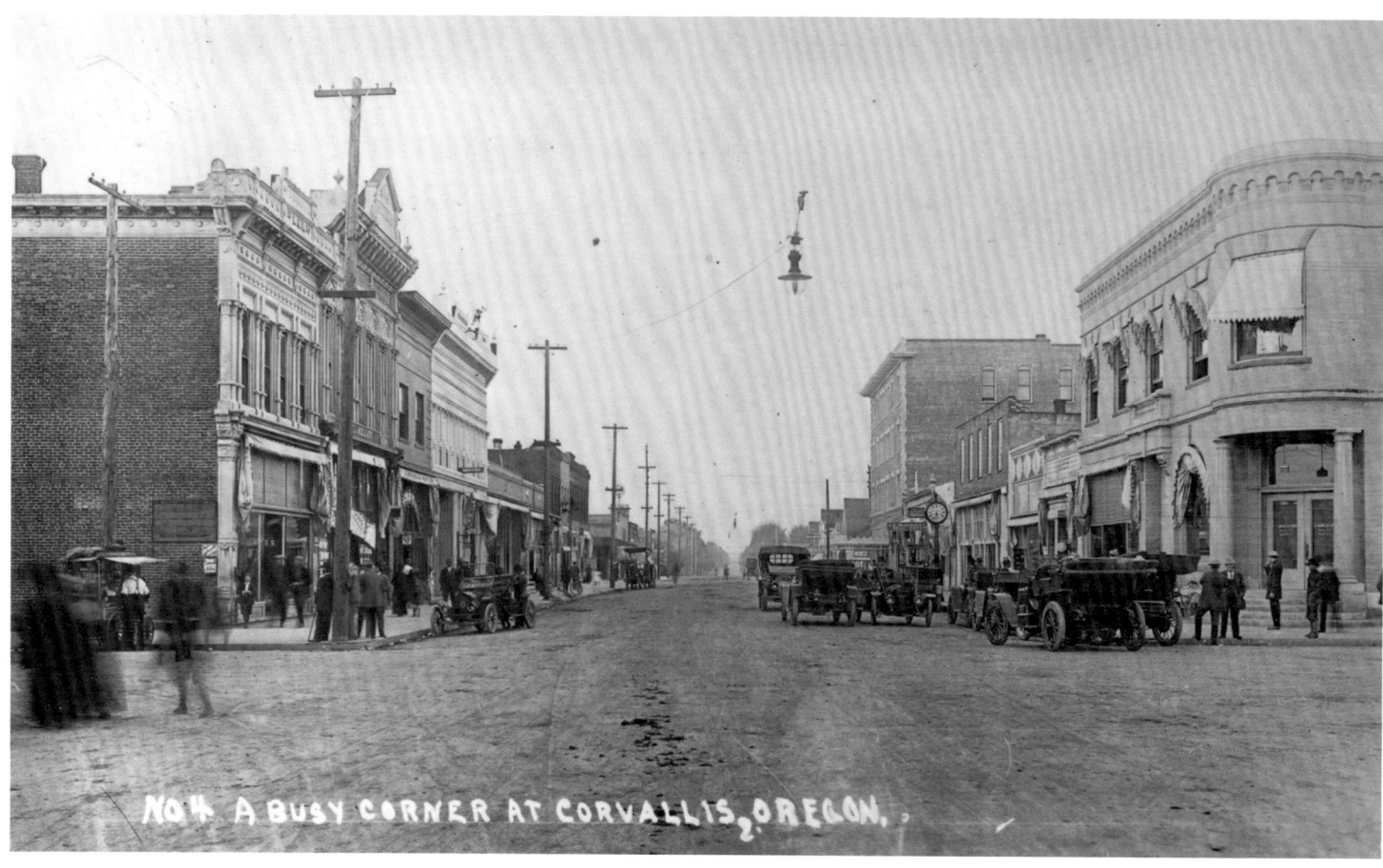

Second Street, looking north from Madison, Corvallis, ca. 1915 (OHS Neg. OrHi 85350)

Corvallis 1915-1994

Joseph Avery laid out twenty-four-block Marysville in 1848 on the banks of the confluence of the Willamette and Marys rivers. Steamboats started arriving in 1851, bringing people and manufactured goods and exporting produce, furs, and lumber. In 1853 the town was renamed Corvallis, meaning heart of the valley. The Oregon Legislature designated that Corvallis College receive the benefits of federal land grant funds established by the U.S. Congress during the Civil War and an agricultural college was developed. Industry flourished along the river, with flour, lumber, and planing mills, a creamery, and an ice-making plant providing jobs for residents.

Corvallis grew because it was the most southerly ferry landing for men headed to the gold fields in southern and eastern Oregon. It then developed as a regional trading center and became the county seat of Benton County. In the 1880s, after the railroad reached town (1878) and the university was firmly established, the town was a thriving small community.

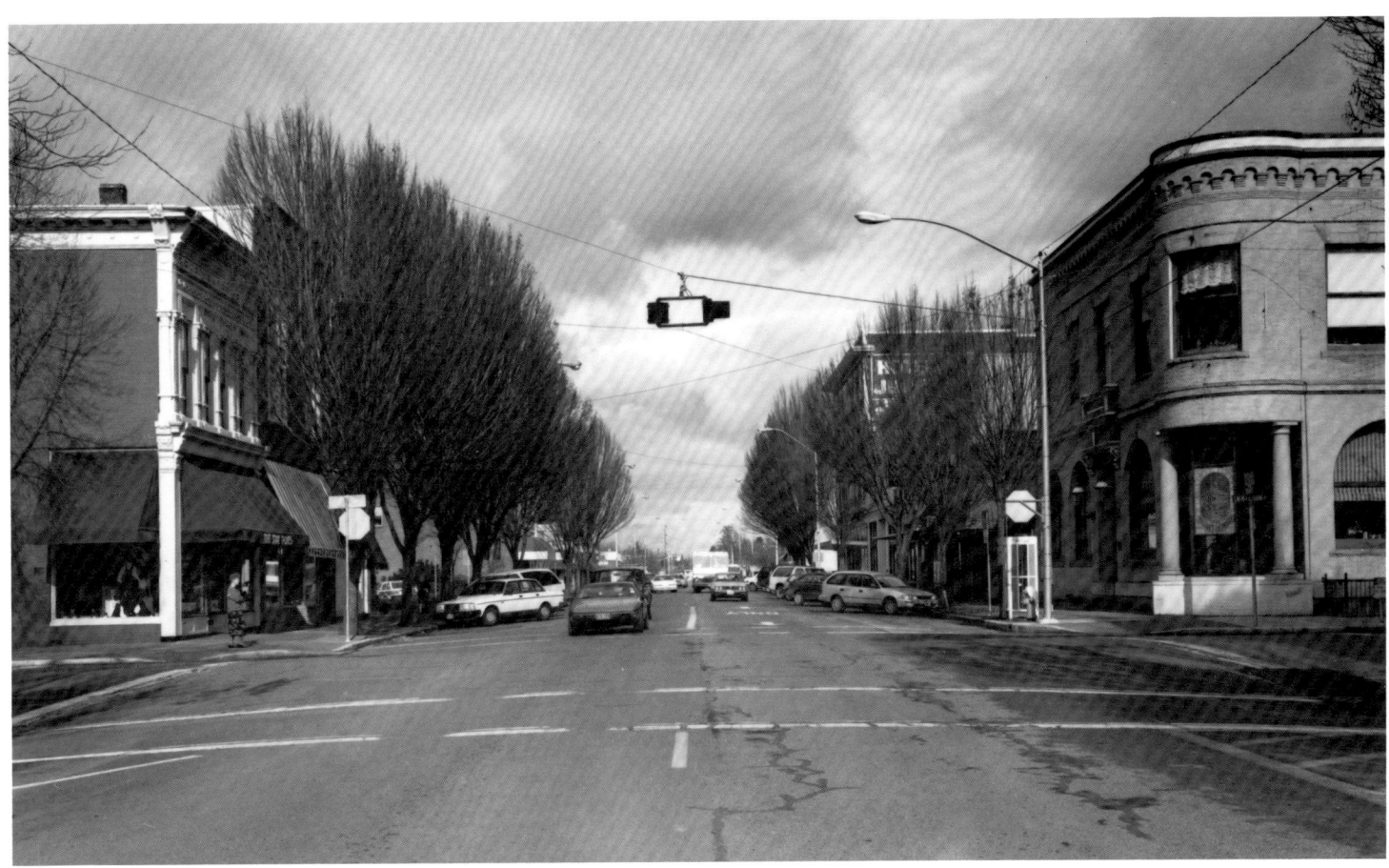

Second Street, looking north from Madison, Corvallis, 1994 (OHS Neg. Lot 824-8)

Second Street was the Main Street of early Corvallis. It has remained a viable commercial street even though the town has branched out beyond the confines of the river. The Kline Building (1889) on the left and the Benton State Bank Building (1910) on the right are very much intact. The Hotel Julian at center left was built in 1893 as a Queen Anne-style building but fell on hard times after the panic (depression) of 1893 and was completely remodeled in 1910 when a simple flat facade replaced and modernized the original facade.

In a typical early 20th century street scene, cars and horse-drawn vehicles are moving helter-skelter in a seemingly random traffic pattern. Cars parked in the middle of the street without much concern, perhaps so their owners could discuss the daily financial news in front of the bank. Note the popcorn stand on the left. It was successfully run by Mr. Bullis, whose descendants still live in Corvallis. The hornbeam street trees, though deciduous, block the view of the front facades of the buildings year round. They were planted in the 1970s as a downtown beautification project.

Eugene 1890-1994

Euro-American claim to the area now called Eugene was established in 1847 when Eugene F. Skinner established his claim close to a butte near the Willamette River (Skinner's Butte is visible in the middle background of the historic photograph). The town was platted in 1852 and became the seat of the newly-formed Lane County in 1853. That same year a public square was dedicated at Eighth and Oak to accommodate new public buildings. The first steamboat arrived on the Willamette in 1857, followed fourteen years later by the railroad. The University of Oregon was established in 1876 and the town grew steadily to become the third largest city in Oregon.

With its towers and Queen Anne-style architecture, the Lane County Bank Building (1888), is visible on the left of the historic photograph. Amazingly, it was torn down by 1916 because of financial difficulties. The three-story Smeede Hotel (1885) located to the middle right of both photographs is the only intact survivor common in both photographs. In the 1960s and 1970s, urban renewal hit Eugene with a wrecking ball. Many historic buildings were destroyed to make way for larger, more efficient civic and commercial buildings to accommodate the town's growth. Citizens rallied to save the Smeede from demolition in 1973 and were also able to save the four-story Tiffany Building (1913).

The cement bollards visible in the current photograph are part of the Eugene Mall (1971), designed to make the downtown more pedestrian-friendly by blocking automobile traffic on Willamette Street. However, the Parcade Parking Structure (1977) demonstrates the continued importance of the automobile in 20th-century Eugene.

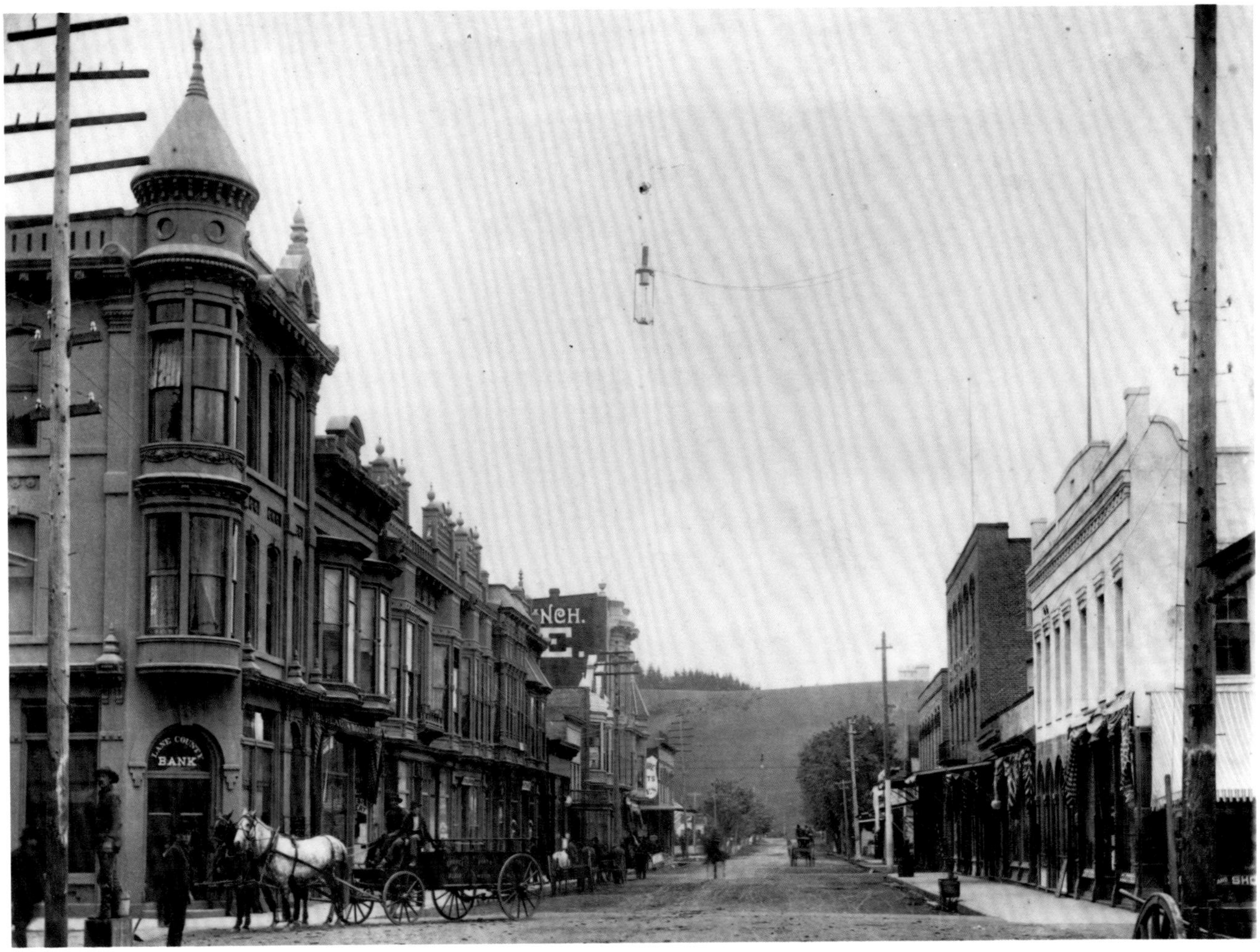

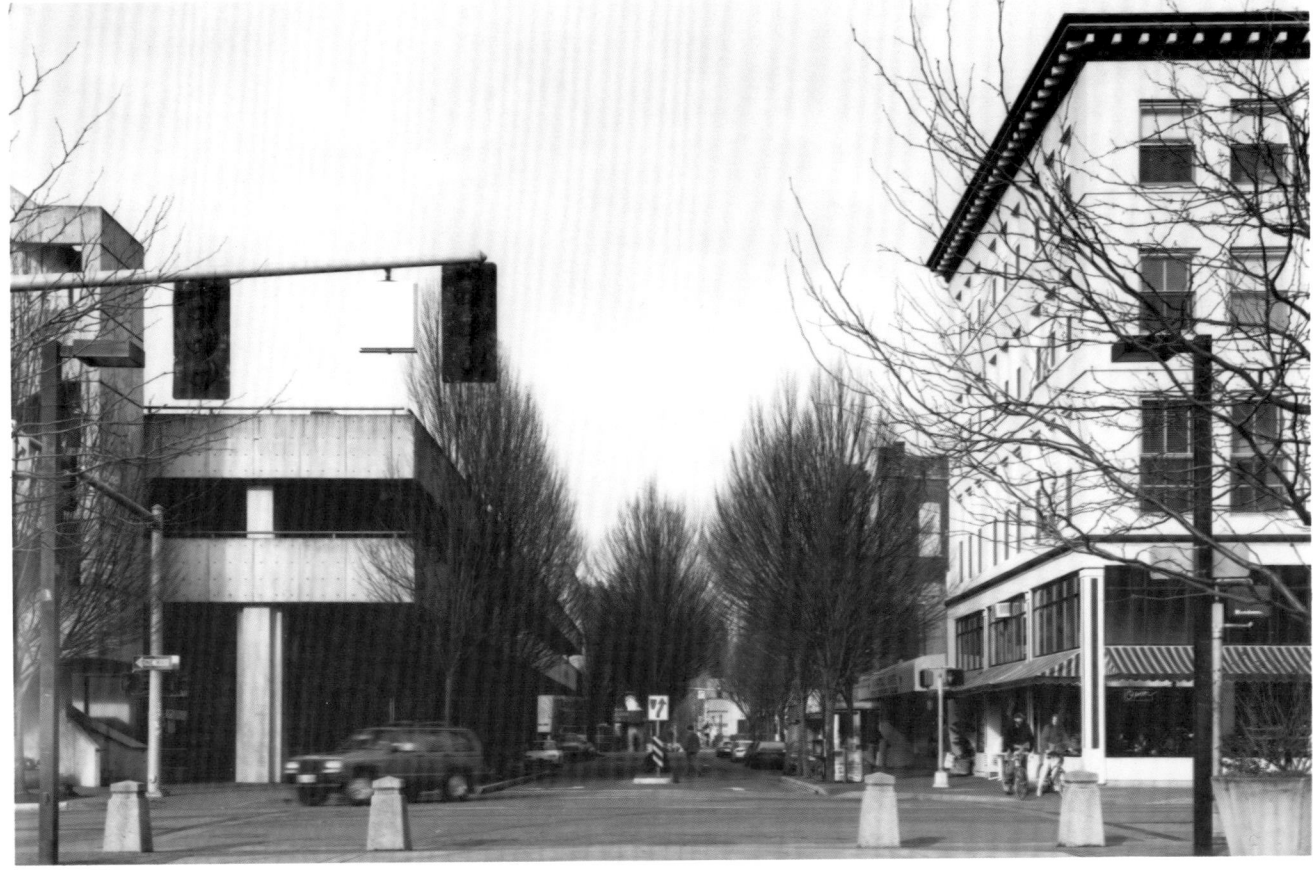

Willamette Street, looking north from 8th, Eugene, ca. 1890 (OHS Neg. OrHi 24889)

Willamette Street, looking north from 8th, Eugene, 1994 (OHS Neg. Lot 824-9)

Astoria 1930-1994

Established in 1811 by fur traders sent by John Jacob Astor, Astoria has the distinction of being the oldest settlement on the Pacific Coast. Nonetheless, the town's early days were not flourishing and it was considered by most to be Astor's greatest business failure. By 1841, Astoria had a scant dozen log houses and five years later the entire population was only thirty inhabitants. Incorporated in 1856, the hilly, isolated location continued to retard the town's growth, and not until the late 1870s was there a real growth spurt, driven by the success of the salmon canneries. Large Victorian residences were erected during this economically successful era. When the salmon industry declined after the turn of the century, the town experienced an economic slump and again growth was halted.

In 1922 a major fire which started in a building near the left center of these photographs destroyed a thirty-two block area of the downtown. The town was immediately rebuilt, with the historic infrastructure replaced by new 20th-century technology incorporating modern underground wiring, wider streets, and fireproof buildings.

Most of the buildings constructed in downtown Astoria during the twenties still survive. The Associated Building (c. 1923) center left with parapet walls featuring classic style urns, and the Hotel Astor (c. 1924) which exhibits vertical Gothic Skyscraper elements are but two of the Twentieth-Century Period Revival buildings that give the town its half-modern character.

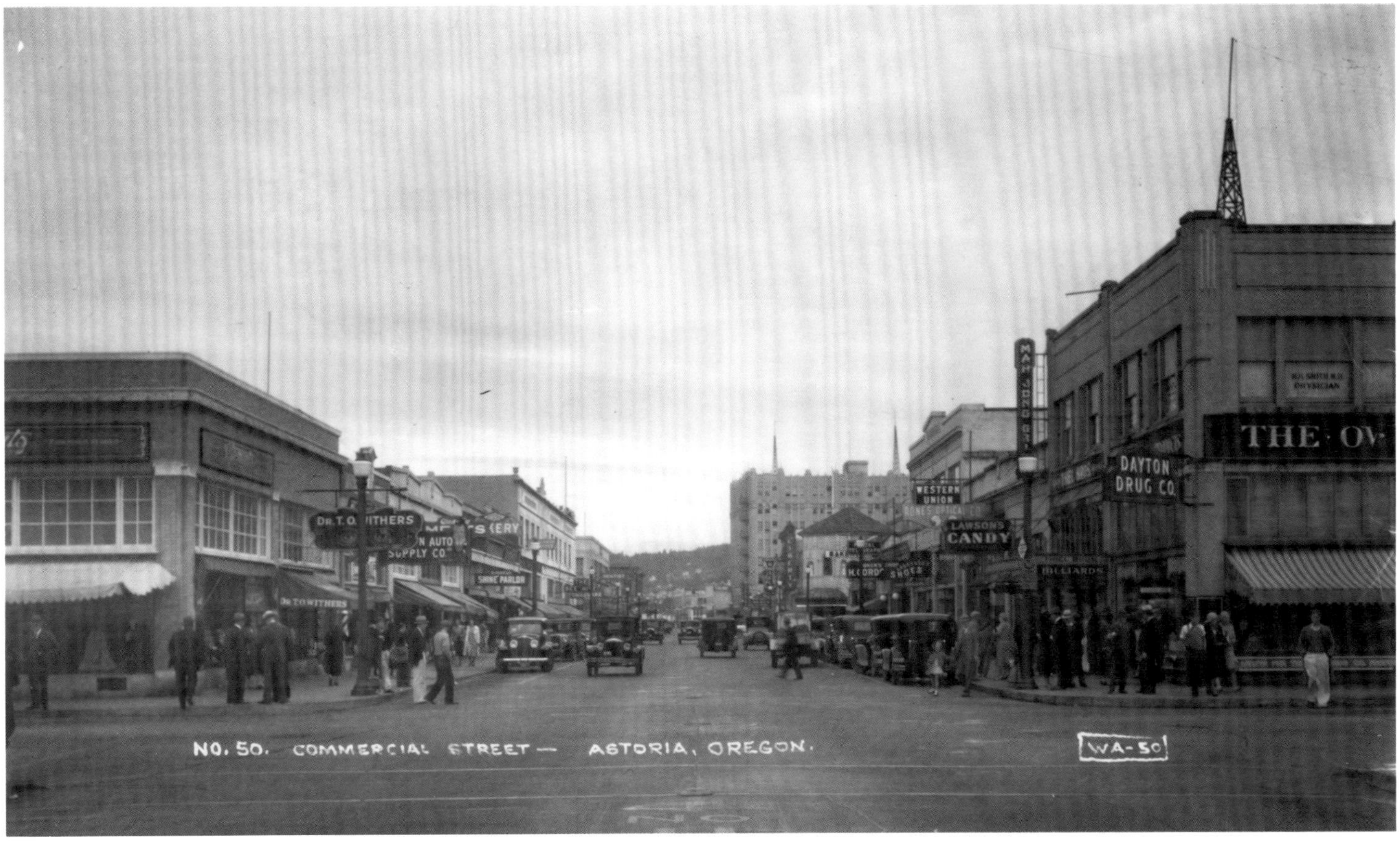

Commercial Street, looking east from 11th, Astoria, ca. 1930 (OHS Neg. OrHi 13786)

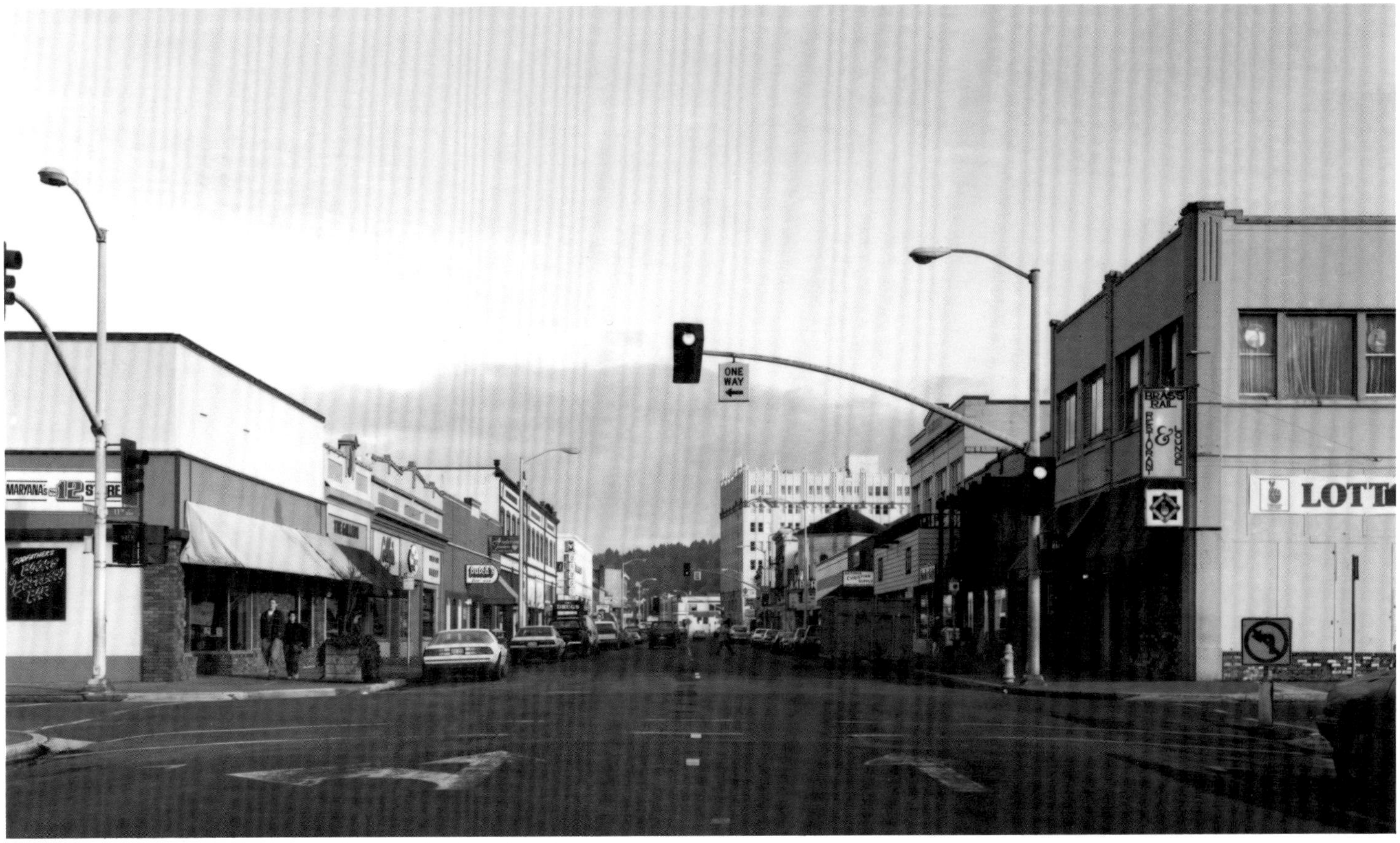

Commercial Street, looking east from 11th, Astoria, 1994 (OHS Neg. Lot 824-11)

Tillamook 1930-1994

Tillamook is named for a large tribe of the Salish Indians (noted as the Kilamox and Killamuck by Lewis and Clark) who inhabited the area before Euro-American settlement began in 1851. The town site was established ten years later and was called Lincoln, Hoquarton, the Landing, and finally Tillamook by 1866. In 1905, the town had a population of 900 people and served as the county seat and commercial trading center for families in the area who lived on the rich farm land, harvested the plentiful Sitka spruce and Douglas fir trees, or fished the nearby bountiful rivers and Pacific Ocean.

Tillamook cheddar cheese is marketed worldwide and the town has become the home of the largest cheese processing plant in the world. The Tillamook County Creamery Association began in 1909 and cheese became its primary dairy product to best utilize overabundant local milk production.

Tillamook was nearly destroyed by fire in 1893 and again in 1905. The historic buildings that remain in the downtown are the unadorned utilitarian commercial brick buildings common to that era. The historic photograph depicts a coastal community somewhat dependent on the tourist trade that journeyed through town on Highway 101 en route to the beach. The signs along Main Street virtually shout for the attention of potential customers to buy automobile products, food, and lodging. The floating sign in the historic photograph says Netarts, Oceanside Beaches (located about seven miles west). The remodeled Tillamook Hotel, center right, is the most apparent survivor from the historic period.

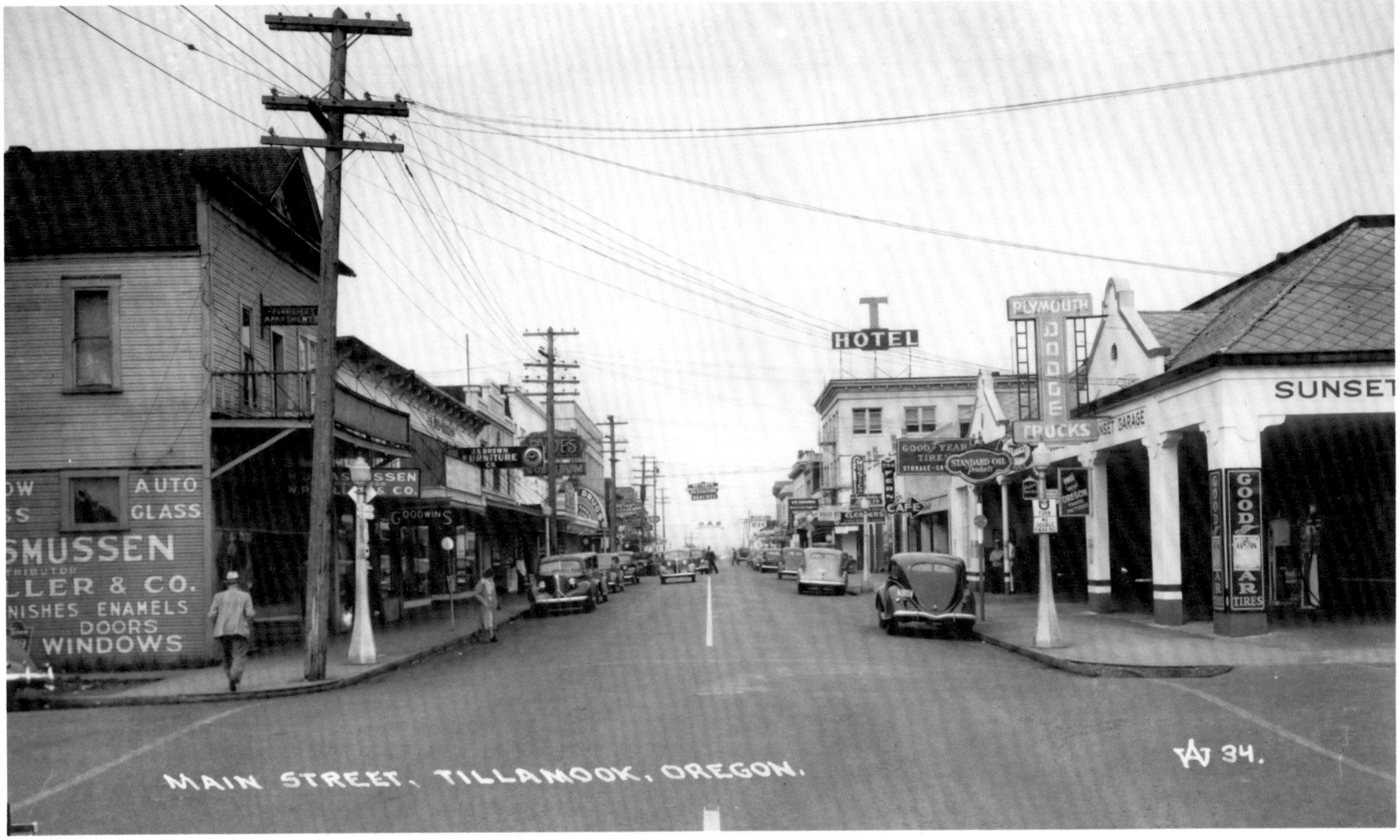

Main Street, looking north from Fourth, Tillamook, ca. 1930 (OHS Neg. OrHi 18478)

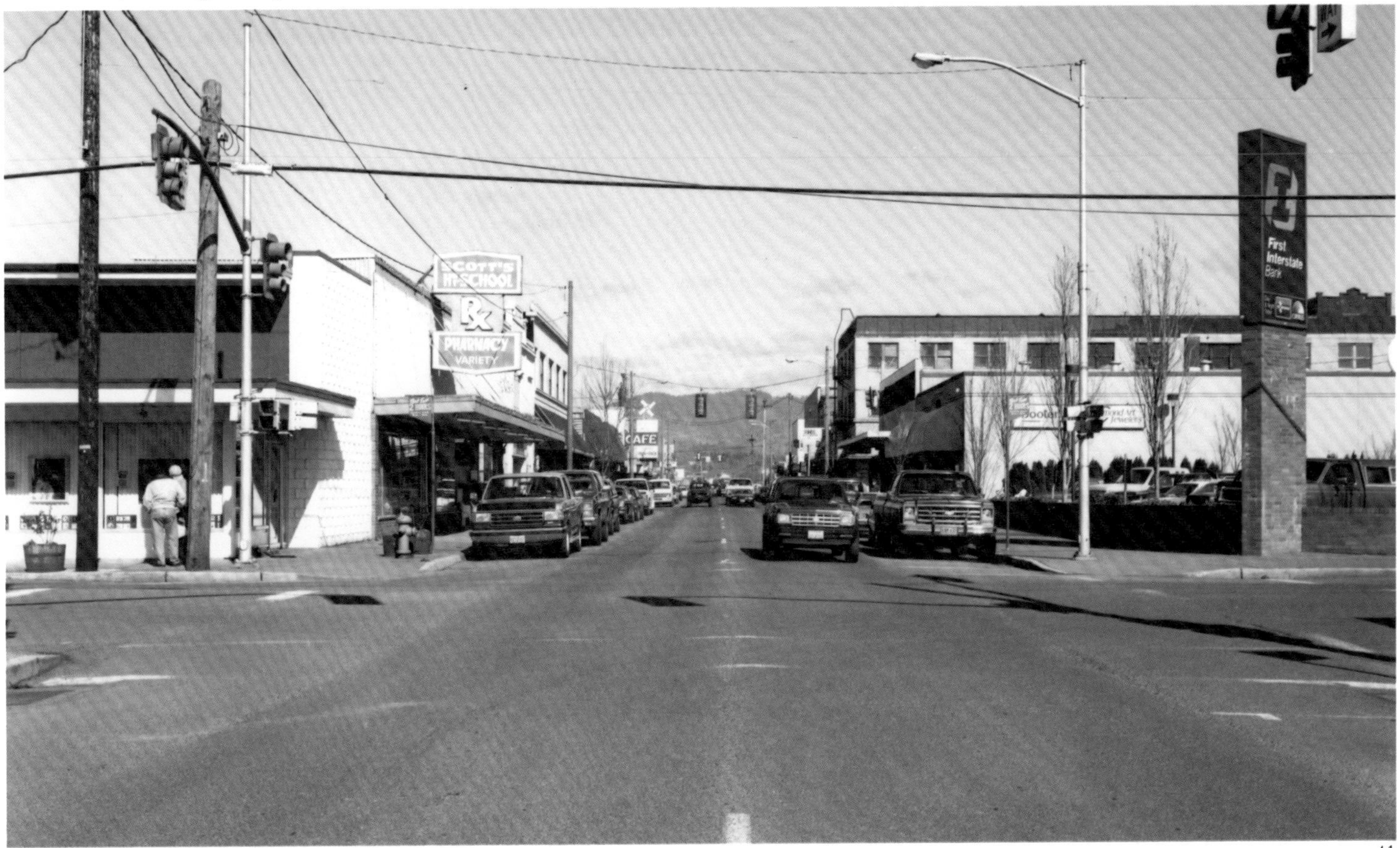

Main Street, looking north from Fourth, Tillamook, 1994 (OHS Neg. Lot 824-12)

41

Newport 1915-1994

This bay front section of Newport was by-passed in the 1930s when the Coast Highway (US 101) was constructed. It is now a separate district of Newport called Old Town, and is a thriving tourist and working fishing community, with art galleries, tourist attractions, and commercial fishing companies operating side by side.

Newport has been the most popular resort town on the coast for mid-Willamette Valley residents since the mid-1860s. Eager to enjoy the cool, refreshing breeze of the ocean, adventurous visitors would get on a coach in Corvallis and travel across the Coast Range by way of the Corvallis and Yaquina Bay Wagon Road, then board a steamboat at Elk City and sail down the Yaquina River to the coast.

The site was originally part of the Siletz Indian Reservation. The area was named Newport in 1864 and opened up to settlement in 1866. Large resort hotels reminiscent of east coast hotels were built and people flocked to the seaside town. The town grew, prospered and was incorporated in 1882. The Corvallis-Yaquina Bay Railroad was completed in 1885 to further boost trade.

The photographs featured show that many of the historic buildings remain but have been altered and covered with new siding to protect the weathered wood. The Yaquina Bay Bridge (1936) seen in the background is one of Oregon's most beautiful arched bridges.

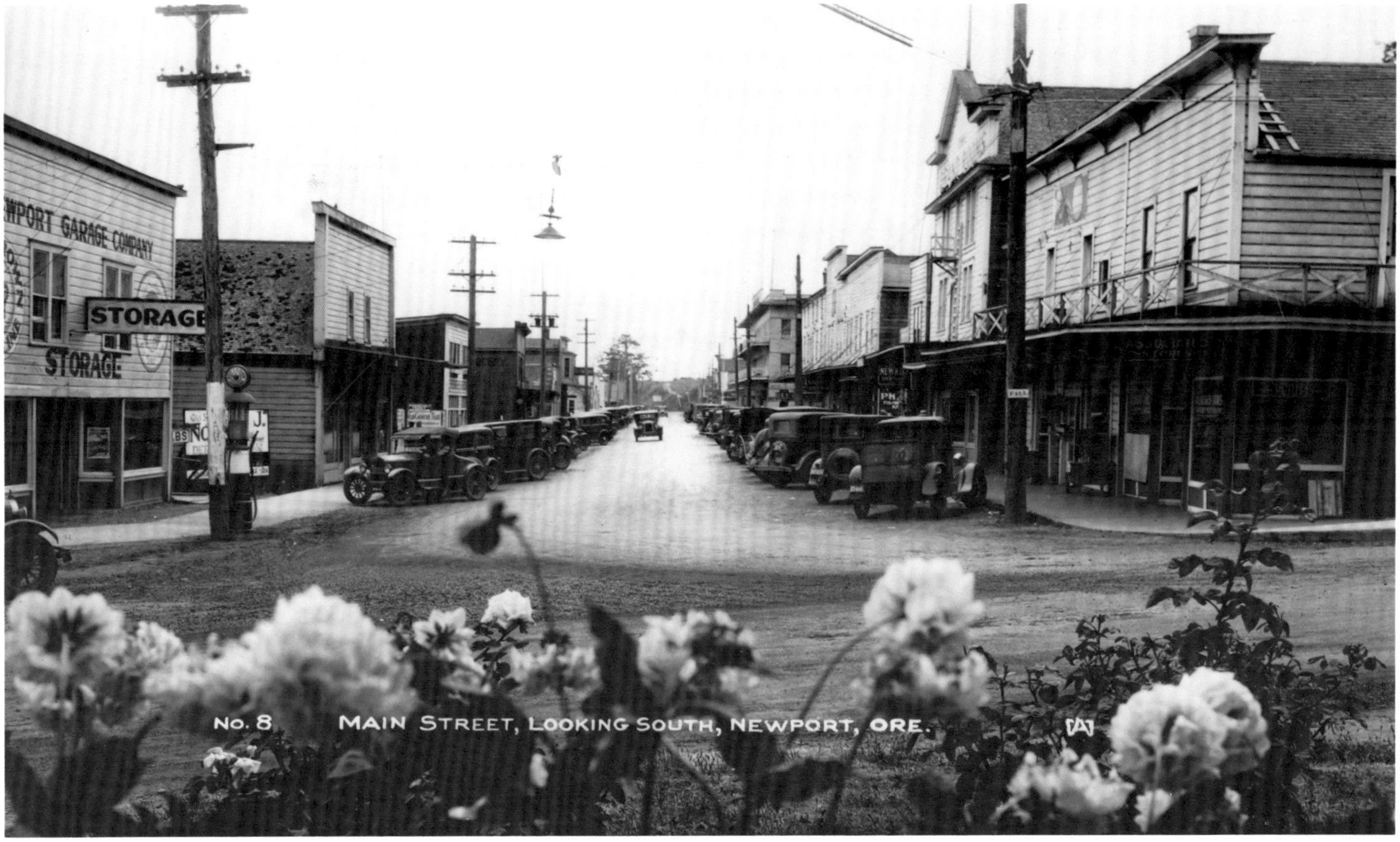

Boulevard, looking west from Fall, Newport, ca. 1915 (OHS Neg. OrHi 16807)

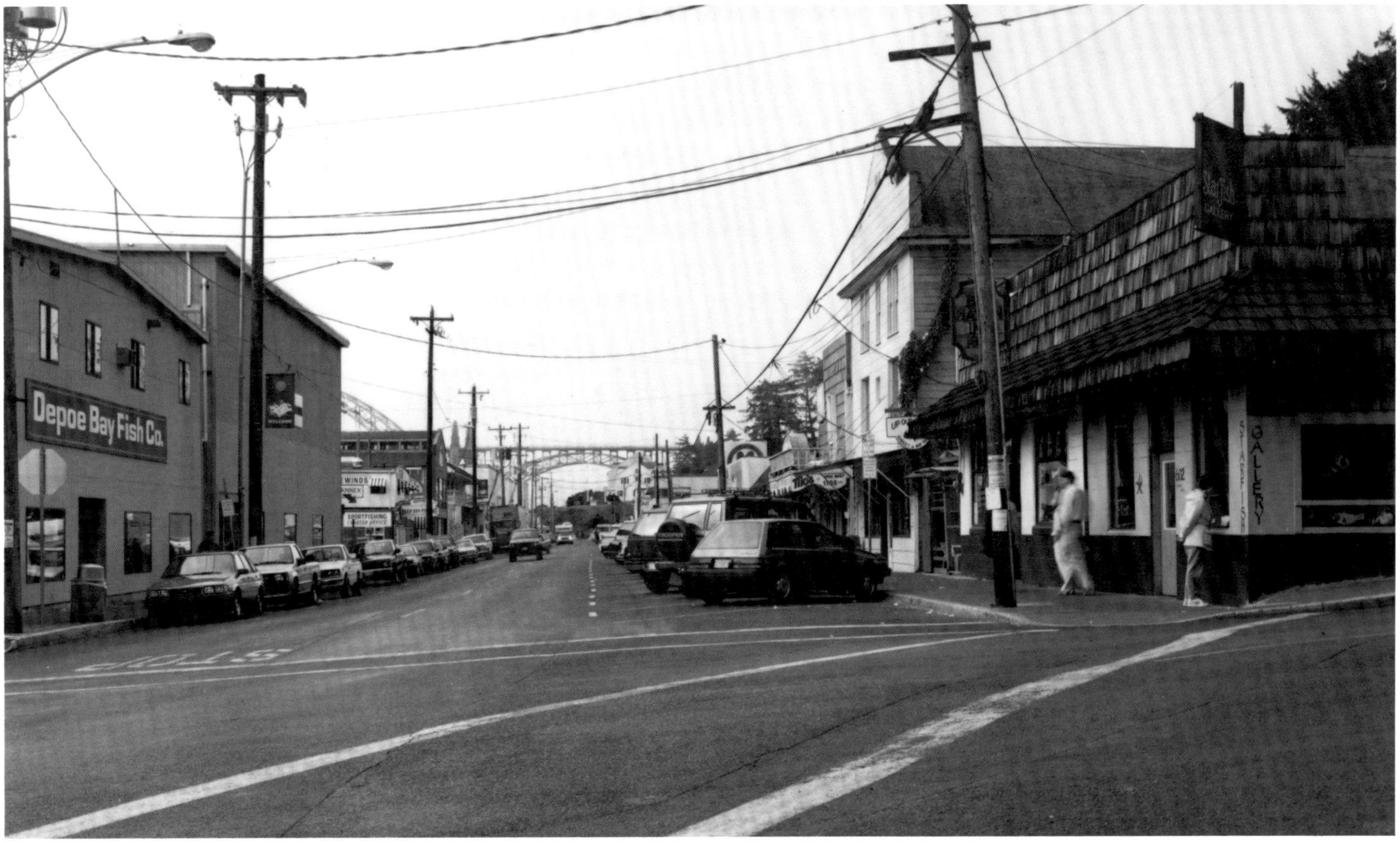

Bay Boulevard, looking west from Fall, Newport, 1994 (OHS Neg. Lot 824-14)

SOUTHWESTERN OREGON

George Kramer

Roseburg　　Medford　　Myrtle Point
Myrtle Creek　　Ashland　　Coquille
Grants Pass　　Jacksonville　　Coos Bay

The southwestern Oregon cities whose main streets are profiled here share, in many ways, a similar history. Isolated for much of the pioneer period from the more populous northern parts of the state, development in this region tended to be slower and less explosive than in the Willamette Valley. Here early wood frame buildings often gave way to brick only following a fire, victims of not economic success, but revised building codes that mandated safer construction. With this slower development, Main Street evolved and often acquired a homogeneity over time. Of course, southwestern Oregon also had its share of boom and bust development. Natural-resource inspired booms, from gold, timber, orchards, and coal each brought a sudden influx of people and wealth to the region. Periodic bursts of construction or widespread renovation can be found in virtually all these towns, and are reflected in these images.

Access to transportation, or the lack of it, was the most significant factor in shaping the character of southwestern Oregon and determining municipal success. This was especially obvious in the early 1880s, when the railroad began working its way south from Roseburg. Existing cities in Josephine and Jackson counties were eager for the economic boost the railroad might bring, and feared being bypassed. In Coos County, which remained isolated from the main line until 1916, access to shipping lanes, either ocean ports, as in Coos Bay, or rivers, as in Coquille, was the deciding factor in community growth.

In the twentieth-century, the rise of the automobile again proved the importance of transportation in southern Oregon. The Pacific Highway, begun in 1913, went through every single Douglas, Josephine or Jackson county main street profiled here except Jacksonville. And in Jacksonville it was the *lack* of transportation access, beginning with the loss of the railroad in 1883, that shaped the community and ultimately resulted in its success as a tourist attraction. On the coast, without a railroad, it was "the smooth wide pavement of U.S. 101 and State 42," which finally succeeded the waterways of the initial settlement period, and served as the basis for community expansion.

George Kramer, M.S., is a historic preservation consultant. He has studied and written widely on the history and development of the cities and towns of Southwestern Oregon.

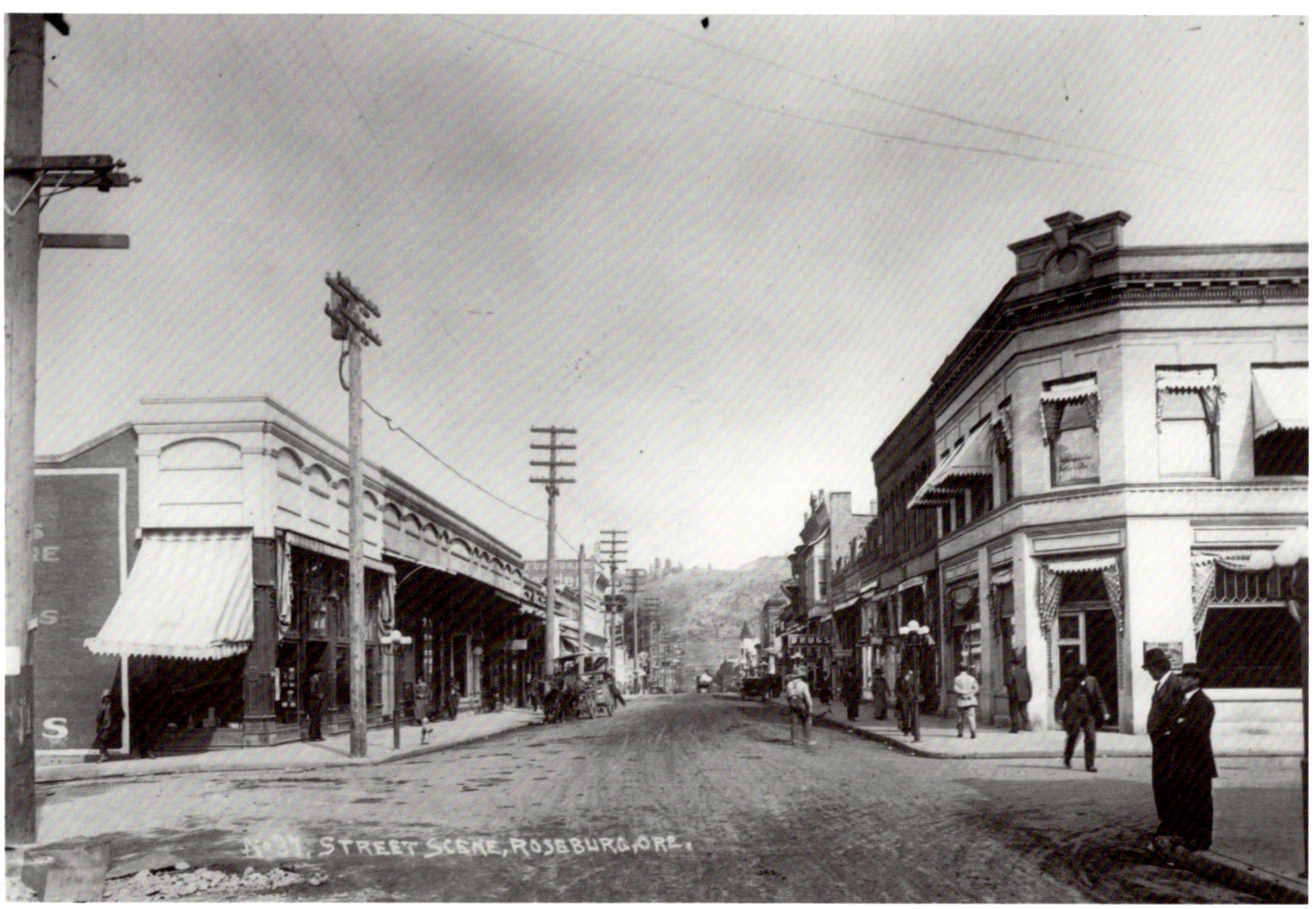

Jackson Street, looking north from Oak, Roseburg, ca. 1910 (OHS Neg. OrHi 36095)

Roseburg 1910-1994

Most of the brick buildings of Jackson Street were constructed between 1890 and 1910, replacing the small wooden buildings that dated from the town's initial settlement in the early 1850s. "Main Streets," such as Jackson, usually mirror the financial and social patterns of the area. As communities grow and prosper, the business community peacocks that success by building, or improving, the town's commercial core.

That was certainly the pattern in Roseburg. The impressive Booth Bank building (1902), on the right, was first the home of a prominent local firm, founded in part by the principals of Booth-Kelley Lumber. As Roseburg grew, so did the bank and their building was first expanded in 1909. In the 1920s the corner entrance gave way to a central columned one and a new facade mimicked a Greek temple — a good "solid" form for banks. Eventually the temple form itself became dated and so, in the 1960s,

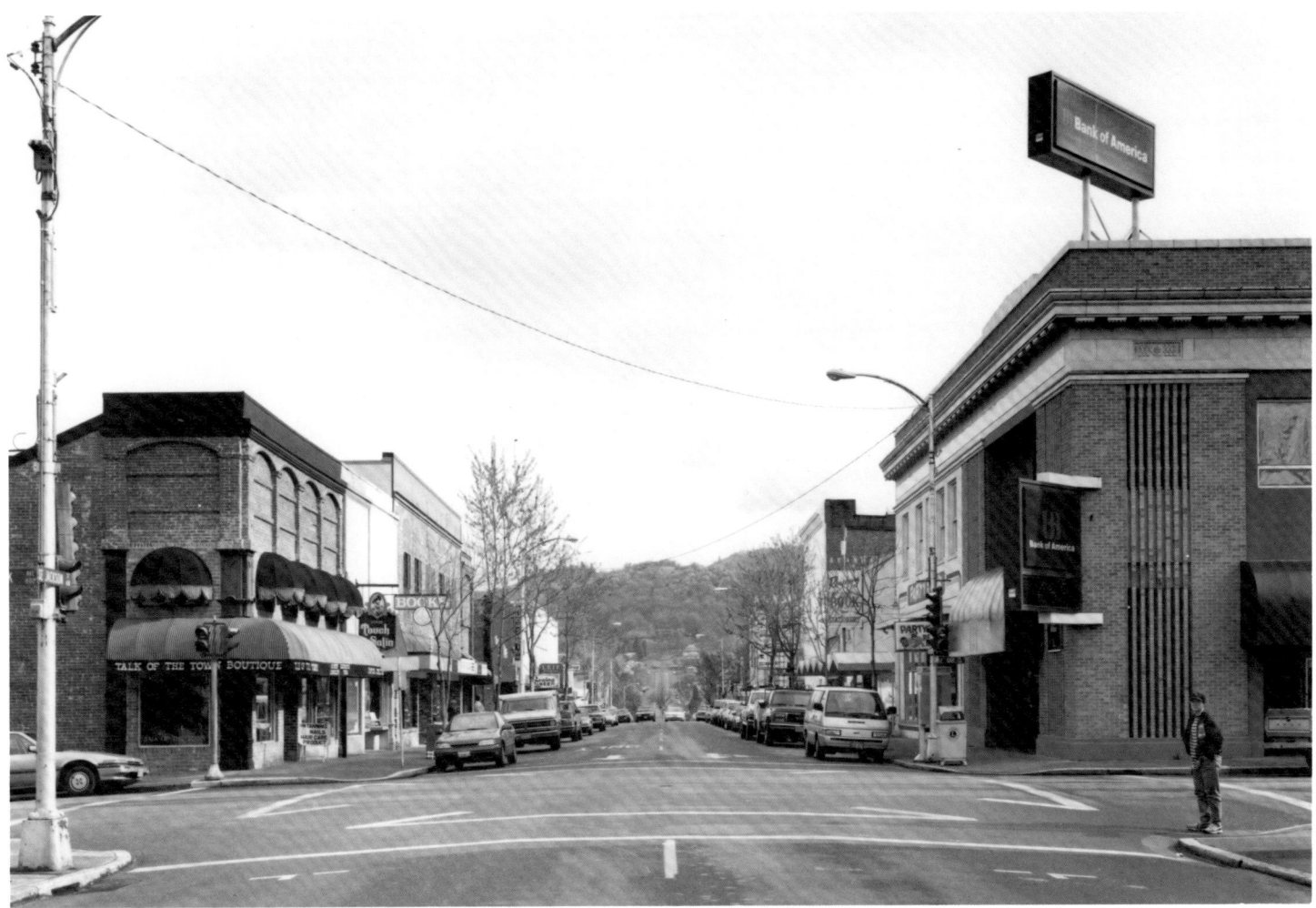

Jackson Street, looking north from Oak, Roseburg, 1994 (OHS Neg. Lot 824-21)

the building was again modernized. The corner entry was rebuilt, this time behind a massive column, and the window bays were filled with two-story high cast-iron "trees." Today the "trees" of the Booth Bank are gone and another institution continues the ninety-year tradition of financial services on this corner.

The cyclical alteration of a facade to accommodate changing taste and use is a typical feature of any economically successful downtown. Rare is the one hundred-year old building that remains exactly as it was built, and those are almost exclusively found in areas that have, in one way or another, failed. In successful towns, merchants and property owners had the funds and drive to keep up with the times. It is only recently that restoration and the return of buildings to more of their original character has come to be timely.

Myrtle Creek 1915-1994

Like most towns located along the Pacific Highway (Highway 99), the steady stream of automobiles that traveled that major route of the western United States played a huge role in the development of Myrtle Creek. First founded in 1868, Myrtle Creek grew slowly in the nineteenth-century, following the boom and bust cycles of the mining and agricultural economy of southern Douglas County. Ringed by mountains, transportation routes beginning with the Applegate Trail, and later the stage and railroad lines were the lifeblood of the city. In 1913, the Pacific Highway was only the latest to pass through town.

The automobile, however, would change the face of small town America as did no previous transportation form. With the growing popularity of automobiles and trucks, cities struggled to accommodate the contraptions. New architectural forms such as garages and gas stations soon became prominent features of Main Street, joining the local bank, the drug store, market, and hotel. The small gas station at the north end of Main Street in Myrtle Creek is typical of such buildings, many little more than small sheds with a huge overhanging canopy to cover the pumps.

In the early years of short driving range and limited reliability, autoists provided a steady stream of business to small town hotels such as the Hotel Myrtle. As cars improved, and traveling distances grew, such hotels faced growing competition from newer, auto-oriented camps that grew along the roadside. These motor hotels, soon called motels, began with small bungalows and car-side convenience. They eventually drove traditional second-floor hotels like the Myrtle out of business. Other Main Street merchants, from the town banker to the local druggist, were prey to the larger firms or national chains that located in larger cities, cities now made accessible by the very automobiles that had defined the life of small towns in the first half of this century. Today, the Hotel Myrtle and the drug store have been replaced by antique and second-hand stores, on the ground floors of buildings with boarded up windows above a street whose primary activity ends along with the workday.

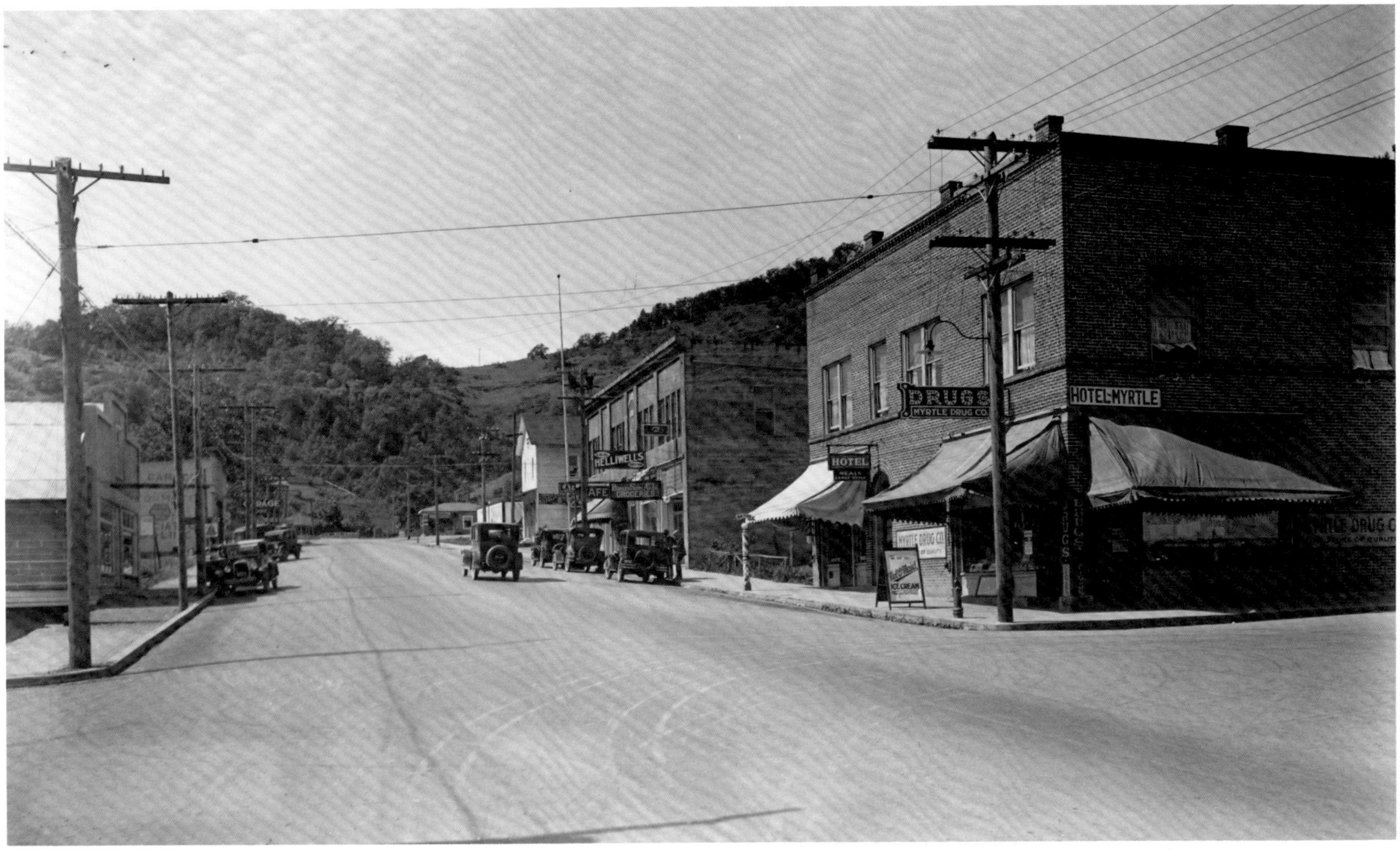

Main Street, looking north, Myrtle Creek, ca. 1915 (OHS Neg. OrHi 50485)

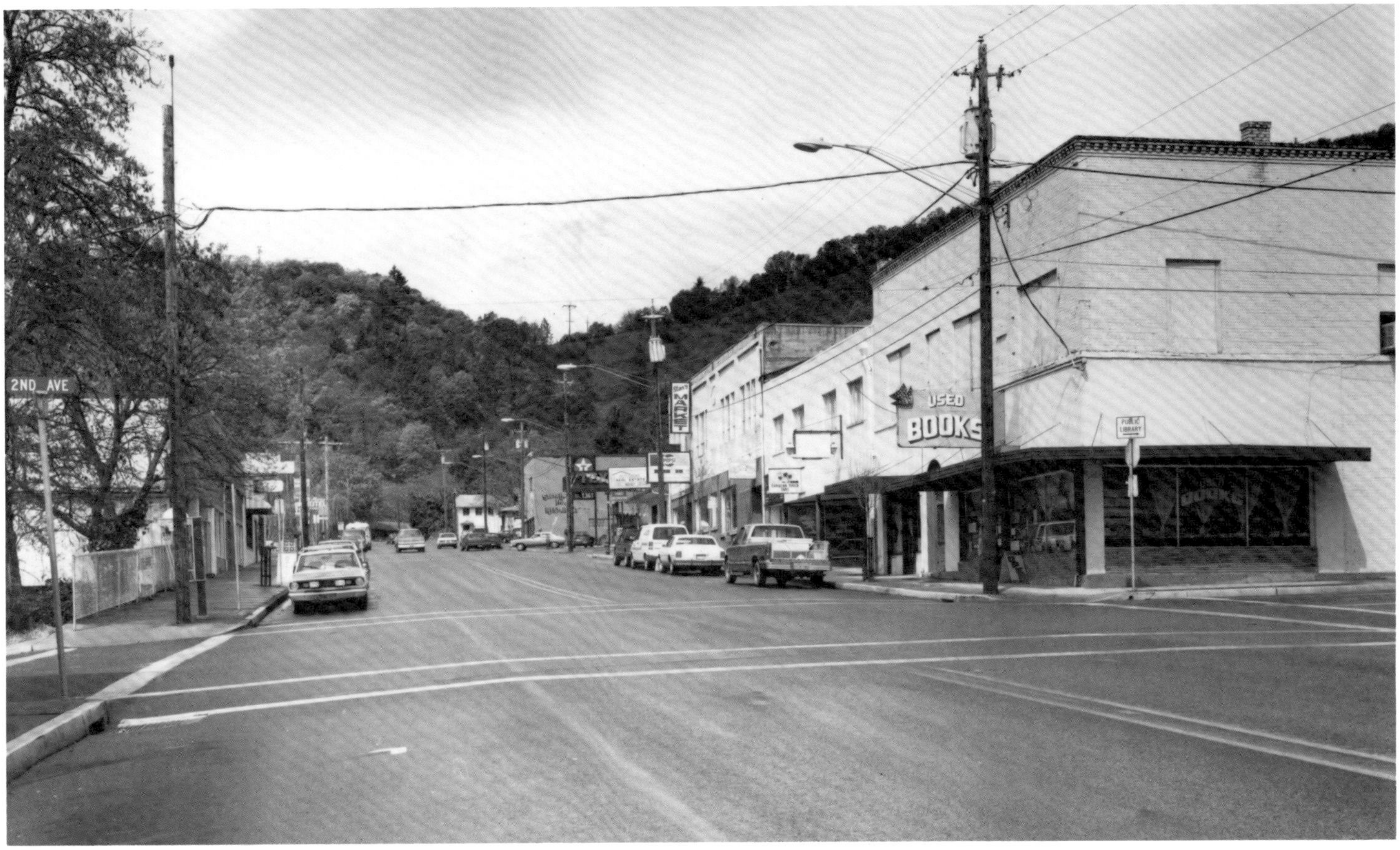

Main Street, looking north, Myrtle Creek, 1994 (OHS Neg. Lot 824-24)

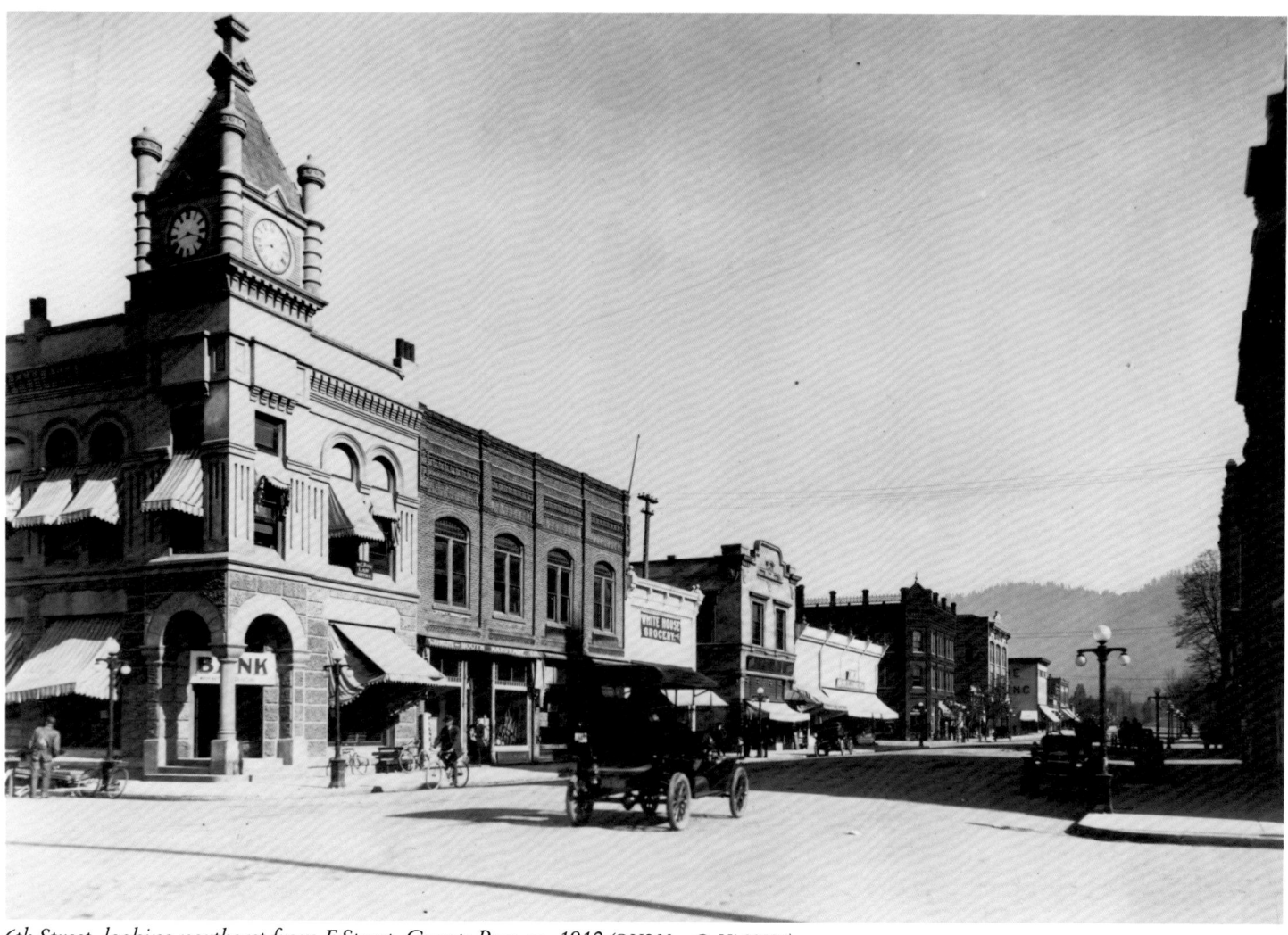

6th Street, looking northeast from F Street, Grants Pass, ca. 1910 (OHS Neg. OrHi 90526)

Grants Pass 1910-1994

Grants Pass was founded in 1883, along with the arrival of the Oregon and California Railroad to the Rogue Valley. Its first main street was G, known as Front since it faced the tracks. Development on Sixth Street, shown here, was substantially hampered by the depot, which partially blocked the street and made through traffic almost impossible. As a result, the first commercial building north of the tracks, the First National Bank Building, wasn't completed until 1890.

In 1893 construction of a new depot, moved out of the roadbed, opened Sixth Street, which quickly overtook G as Grants Pass' main street. Twice as wide, Sixth was far better suited to the automobile and, as that form of transportation bypassed rail after 1910, Sixth Street boomed. The buildings of G Street remained untouched by the prosperity of the postwar years and were recently added to the National Register of Historic Places as elements of the G Street Historic District.

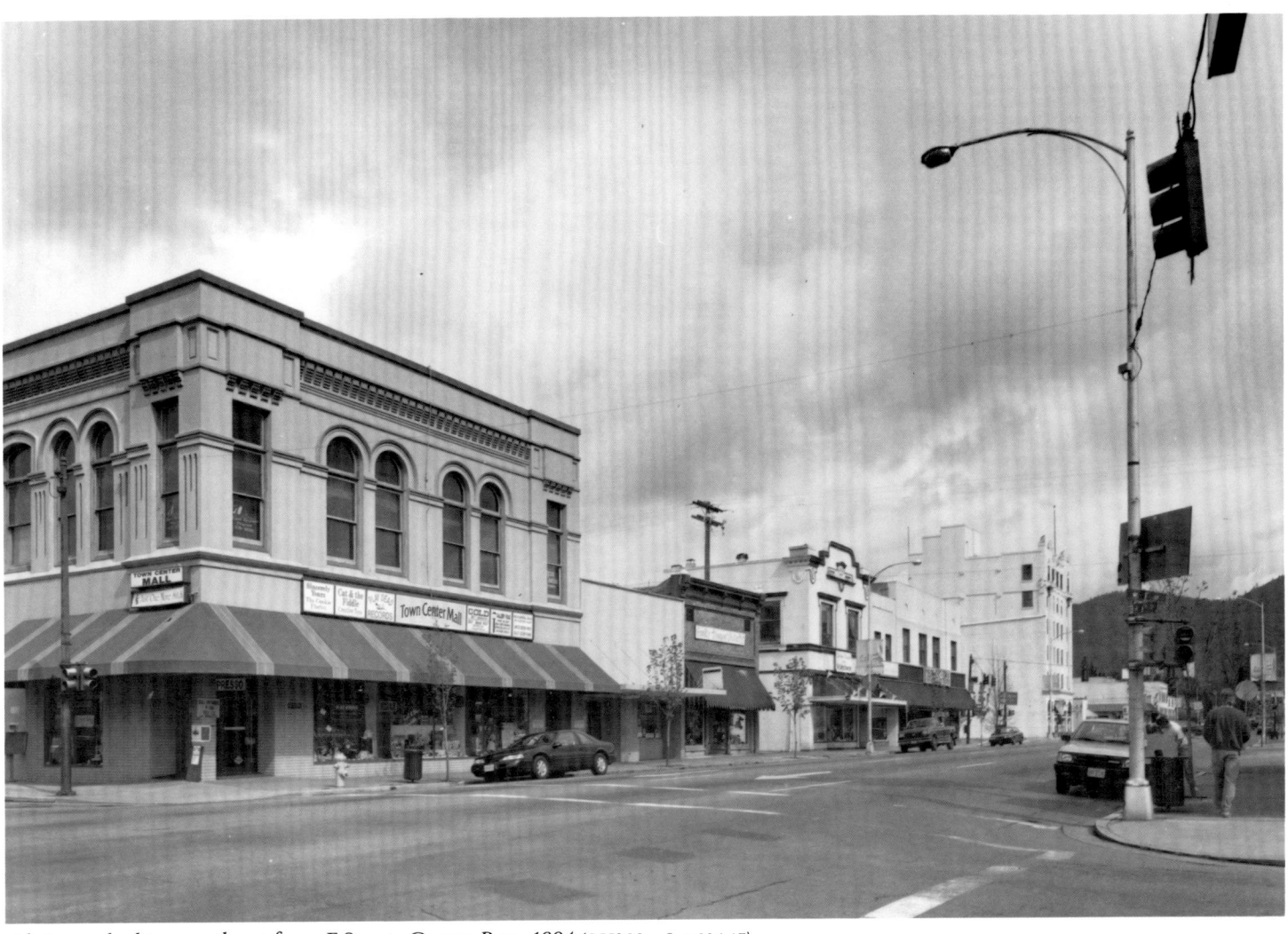

6th Street, looking northeast from F Street, Grants Pass, 1994 (OHS Neg. Lot 824-17)

The structures built facing the more economically successful Sixth Street bear witness to the changing architectural styles of the twentieth-century. Amid the generic remodeled facades and updated storefronts, are the effects of two of the architectural plagues that have hit main streets in the twentieth century. The earlier is the oft-seen "tower-ectomy." In 1926 the First National Bank lost its grand clock tower and its brick and stone exterior was hidden behind a smooth, antiseptic stucco. Such was standard practice as the once landmark feature of a tower became old-fashioned in the "modern" 1920s and 1930s. The second plague, sandblasting, dates from the 1970s, an era which had supposedly begun to rediscover the past. Many a surviving building was unfortunately subjected to such treatment by well-meaning owners whose modern-day sensibilities dictated that all that beautiful brick *must* have been exposed. As the White House Grocery demonstrates, painted appropriately white in the historic photo, such was not often the case.

Medford 1913-1994

Founded by the railroad in 1883, Medford grew into the largest city in southern Oregon following the orchard boom of the first decade of the twentieth century. The city's Main Street was lined with impressive brick and marble buildings that housed the region's financial and professional institutions. Hotels and second floor boarding houses developed for the expanding "drummer" or sales trade, centered around the Southern Pacific depot that dominated downtown. Continued prosperity and growth, and a succession of transportation routes, have put constant pressures on Medford's downtown buildings. Almost all of its blocks have been repeatedly remodeled to reflect changing tastes and uses as the city's merchants kept up with the times.

Some once prominent landmarks like the Nash Hotel were replaced with less imposing modern buildings that dramatically deviate from the historic exuberance of the street. Others, such as the 1902 Palm Building (Rogue River Abstract Co.) still stand but were long ago stripped of their original detailing. Such buildings, dramatically altered prior to World War I, simply reflect Medford's dynamic past and economic vitality.

Until recently, historic preservation all too often needlessly focused on the initial appearance of a building or block, disregarding the important changes that occurred over time. In Medford, no building better represents that continuing pattern of change than the First National Bank. Constructed in 1886, the building was part of a uniform streetscape east of the Nash Hotel. As the historic photo shows, in 1912 the original brick facade was clad with a marble temple-front design. By the 1950s the bank had moved and small retail uses occupied the site. The grand temple front was jack-hammered off and the building was modernized with a huge painted metal panel, highlighted by fourteen-inch diameter concave metal circles. Looking all the world like suction cups, this latest remodel of the First National Bank building is today approaching historic status itself and provides the name by which most Medford residents know the 108-year old structure; the "Bathmat" building.

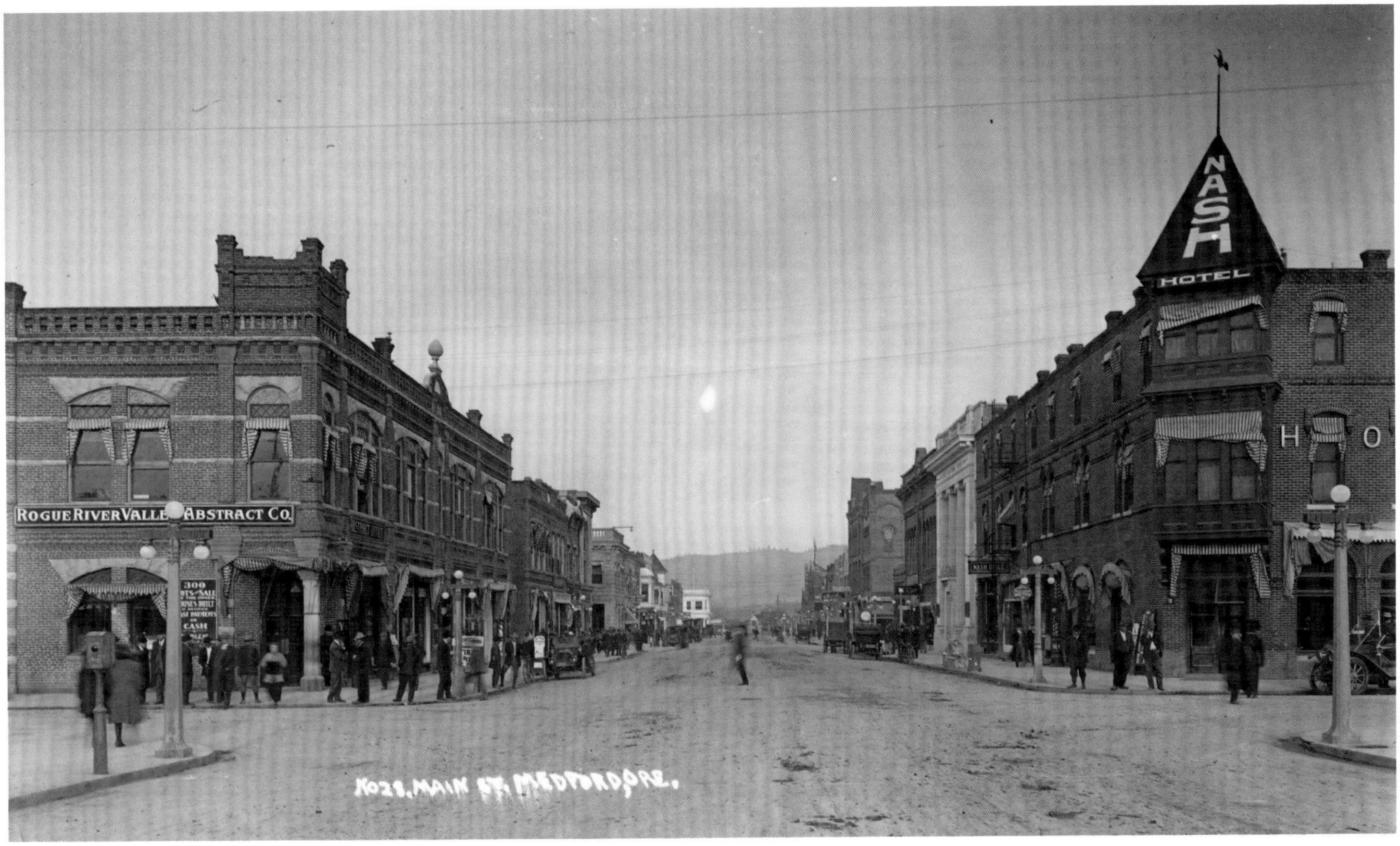

Main Street, looking east from Front, Medford, ca. 1913 (OHS Neg. OrHi 6645)

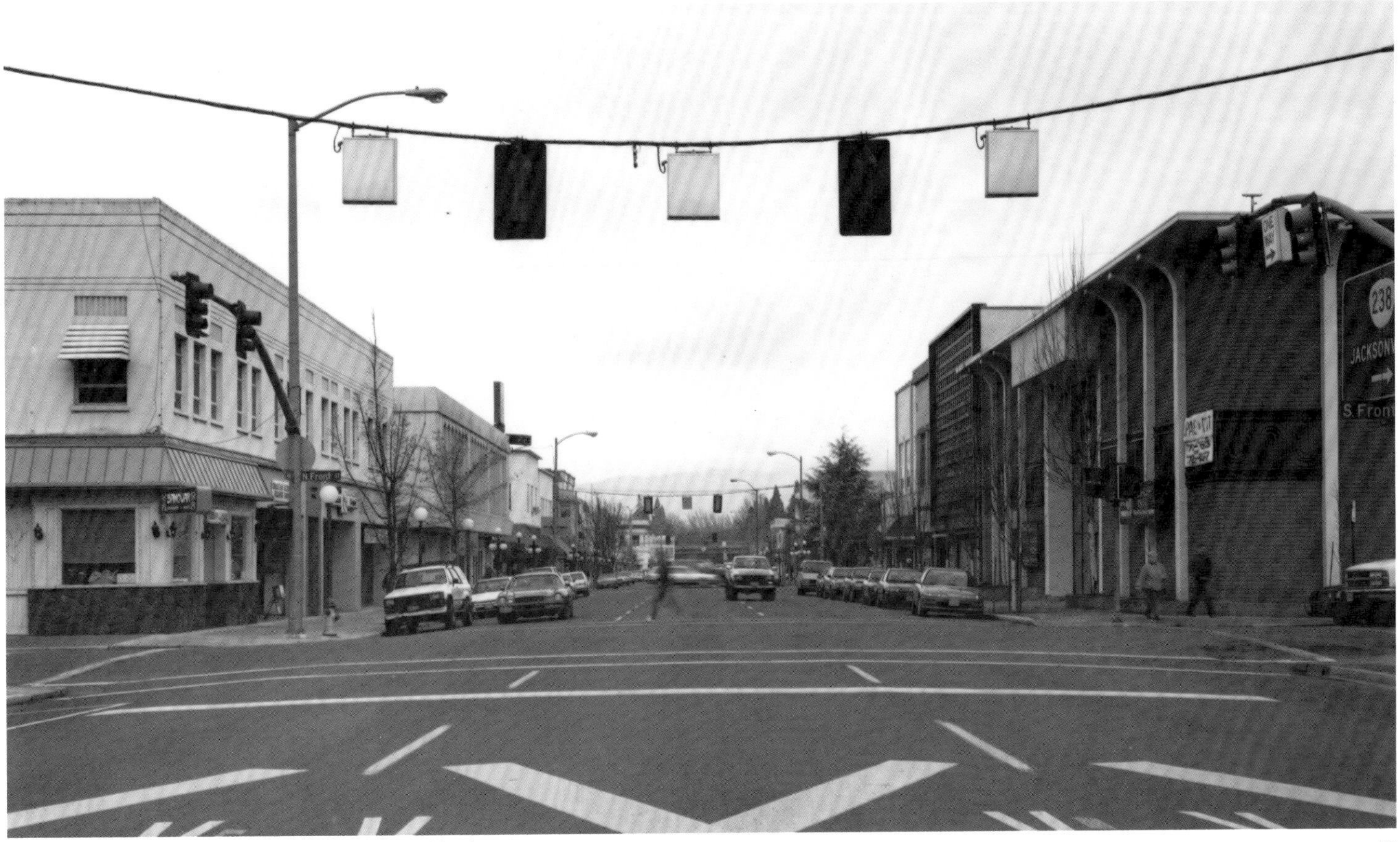

Main Street, looking east from Front, Medford, 1994 (OHS Neg. Lot 824-23)

Ashland 1935-1994

Before the success of the Oregon Shakespeare Festival made Ashland's retail spaces so expensive, many of the commercial icons of a typical small town could be found along Main Street. J.C. Penney, local grocery, drug, and hardware stores, as well as gas stations, were all located right in the heart of Ashland, each gleefully boasting their locations with large neon signs. Today, the growth of the tourist industry and the skyrocketing rents it engenders have driven most non-tourist based businesses to less trendy and less expensive areas of the city.

Despite this dramatic change in use, downtown Ashland has managed to retain a strong sense of its history. Supportive property owners and strong local planning has led to a successful restoration program. Only two buildings in this block, the Lithia Theater and the gas station, have been razed over the past thirty years. But that's not to say things haven't changed. Like many cities, Ashland's appreciation of the past did not extend to its neon signs. An intrinsic visual element in downtown after 1930, neon was often removed following a business change, or as required by city code, which prohibited it after 1967.

The buildings of these two views of Main Street are remarkably similar. But the overall character of Main Street today, shed of its boisterous and prolific signage, lacks the vibrancy and exuberance that it did in the 1930s. For many, there is no reason a restored or historic downtown should be so accurate as to include the rampant commercialization that characterized much of America's pre-World War II cities and towns. Such a view is just one of the blurry lines between preservation and revitalization as it impacts Main Street. In Ashland, the long-standing anti-neon campaign is wavering. The city's small handful of early signs are gaining new recognition and protection as historic elements themselves.

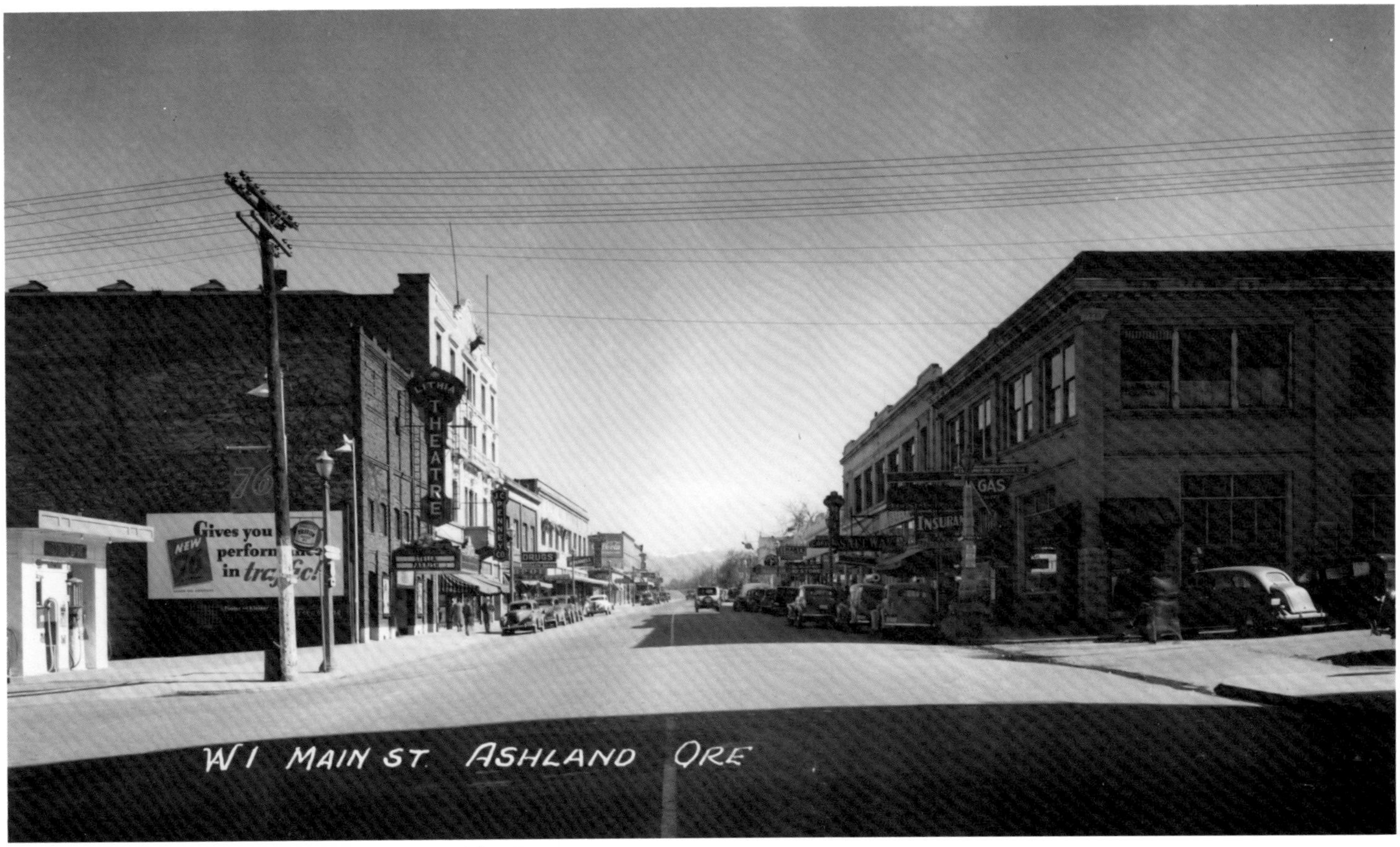

E Main Street, looking southeast from 1st, Ashland, ca. 1935 (OHS Neg. OrHi 13756)

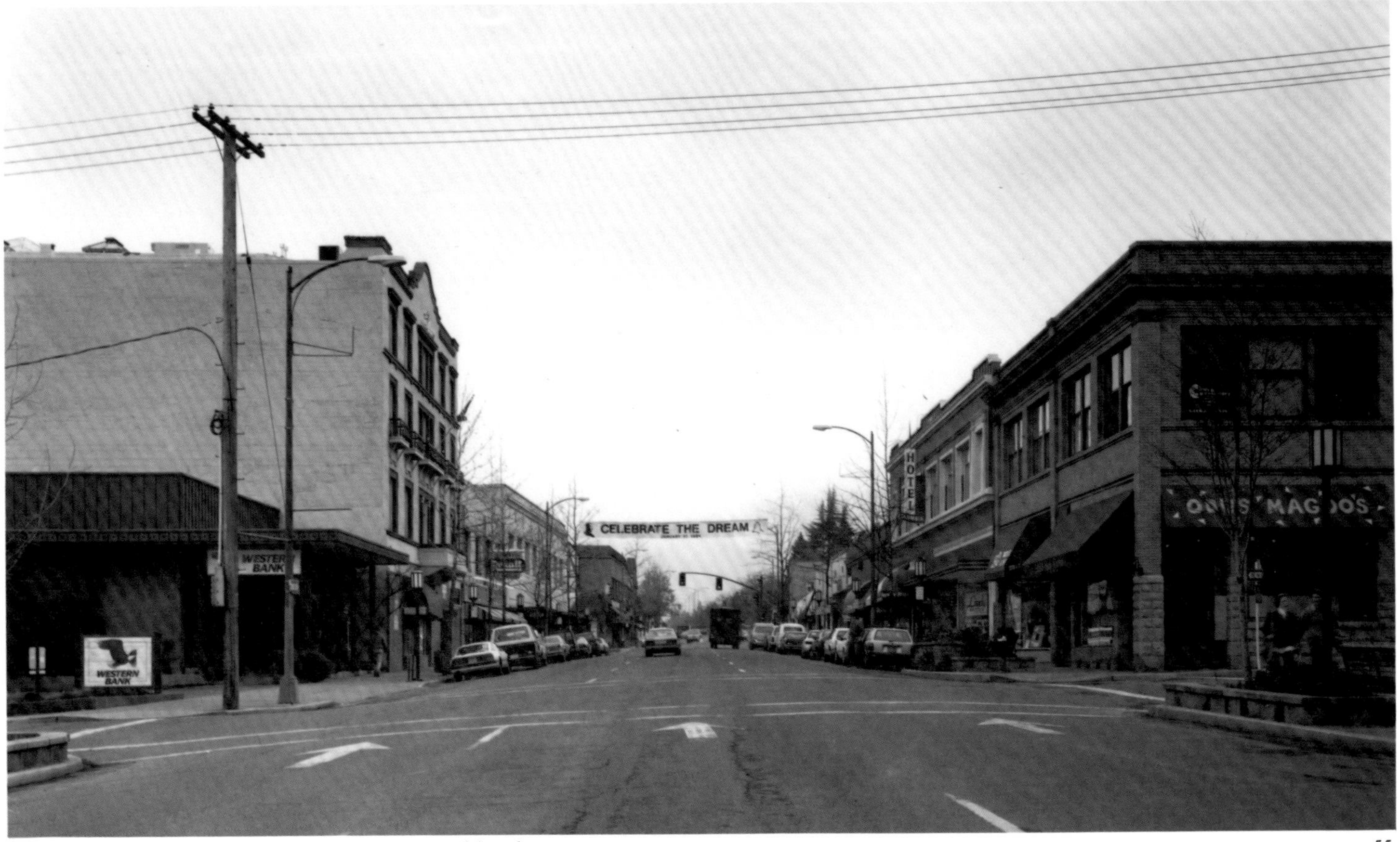

E Main Street, looking southeast from 1st, Ashland, 1994 (OHS Neg. Lot 824-20)

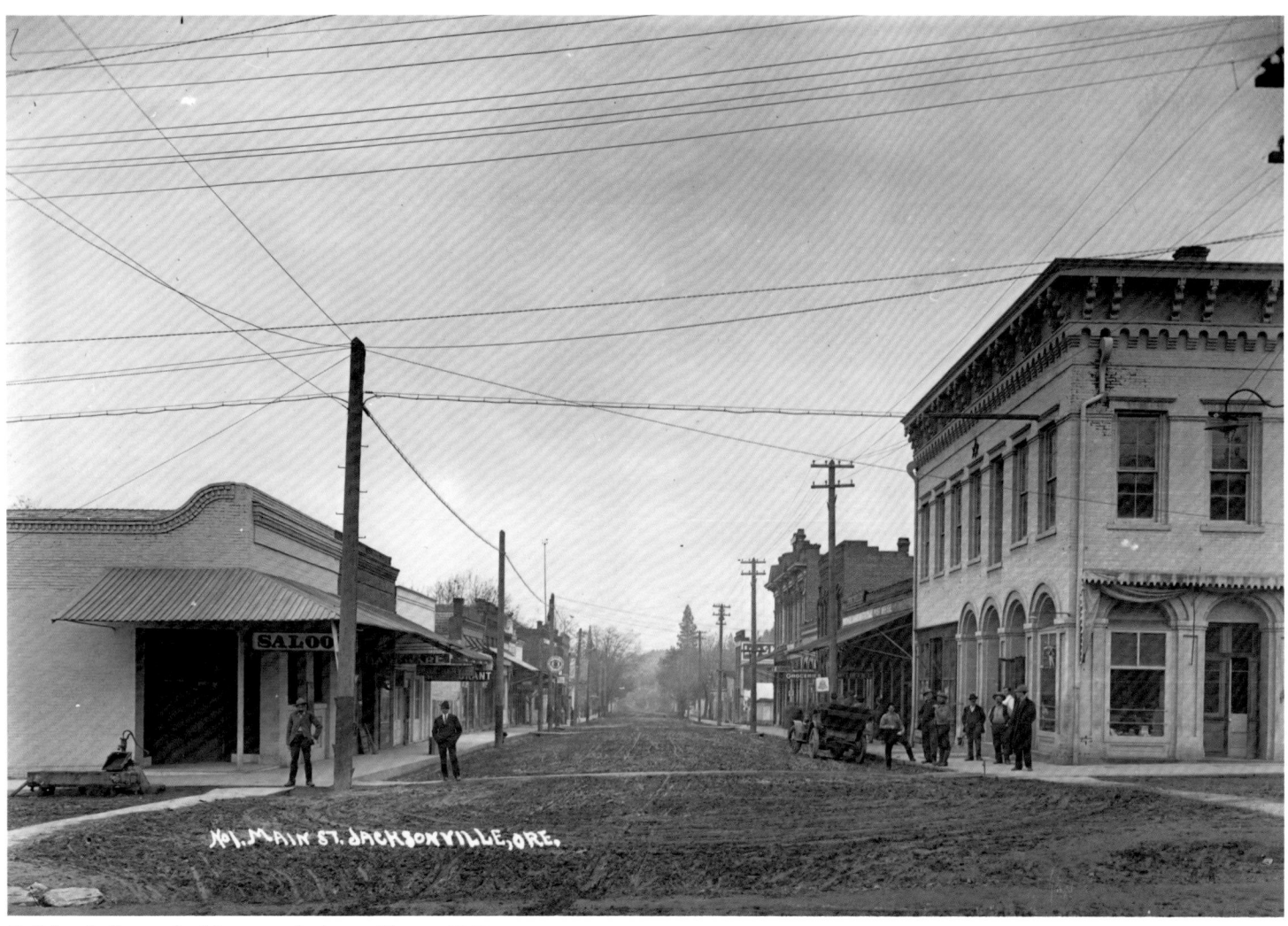

California Street, looking east, Jacksonville, ca. 1910 (OHS Neg. OrHi 15953)

Jacksonville 1910-1994

In the nineteenth century, Jacksonville fancied itself the "Queen City of Southern Oregon" and, as the Jackson County seat, the mining-based town was the largest and wealthiest of the area's communities. On California Street, impressive brick buildings, many dating from the 1860s, were augmented by elaborate 1880s and 1890s structures that peacocked the city's wealth and prominence. Bypassed by the railroad in 1883, Jacksonville began a relentless decline in the last decade of the nineteenth century. Isolated from transportation routes, the city's industrial base died and its population dwindled. Many merchants moved their stores to Medford and new construction ended. The final blow came in 1927, when the county seat itself was moved to Medford, the upstart community on the main rail line.

By the 1930s, much of Jacksonville was abandoned, left for back taxes during the Depression, and the dreaded term ghost town was heard. However, with no economic pressure to modernize, Jacksonville's main street survived the first half of the twentieth century untouched and the county housed its unemployed in the abandoned

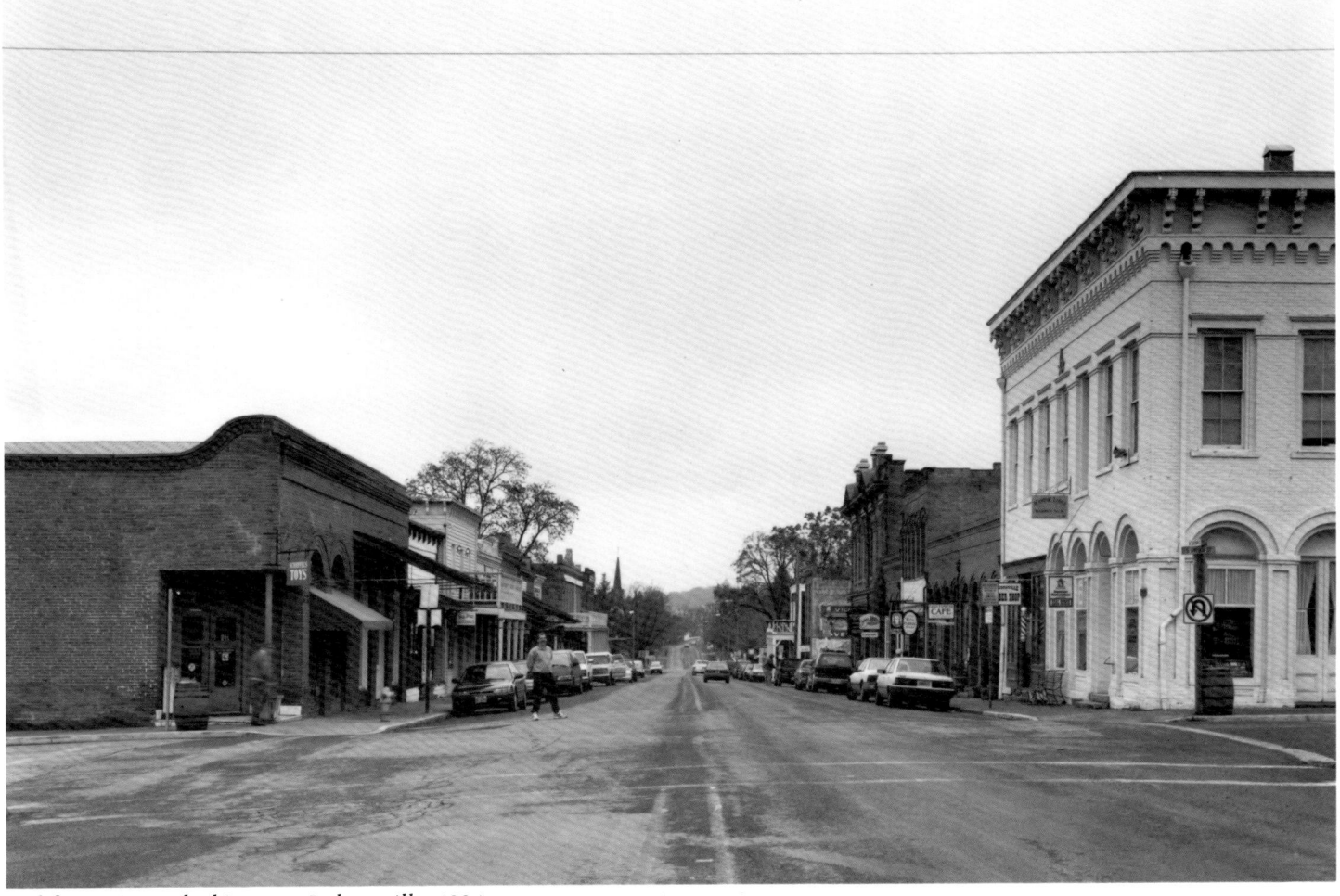

California Street, looking east, Jacksonville, 1994 (OHS Neg. Lot 824-25)

buildings. After World War II, amid growing middle-class residential interest, Jacksonville's commercial buildings and nineteenth-century houses passed from being out-dated to historic as appreciation grew for their surviving character and charm. Restored and refurbished, preservation became the standard method of construction in Jacksonville as once prominent structures were returned to their former glories. In 1966 much of Jacksonville was designated a National Historic Landmark.

Today, Jacksonville's historically pristine streets serve a buoyant tourist economy, providing tangible evidence that history can be good business. But Jacksonville's unsullied quality has, to a degree, been counterproductive to preservation in other southern Oregon communities. Towns that unfavorably compared their own oft-modernized nineteenth century buildings to the brick blocks of California Street can often believe they have little that is historic left. Of course, few cities would wish to go through the economic drought that Jacksonville did that kept its merchants from modernization.

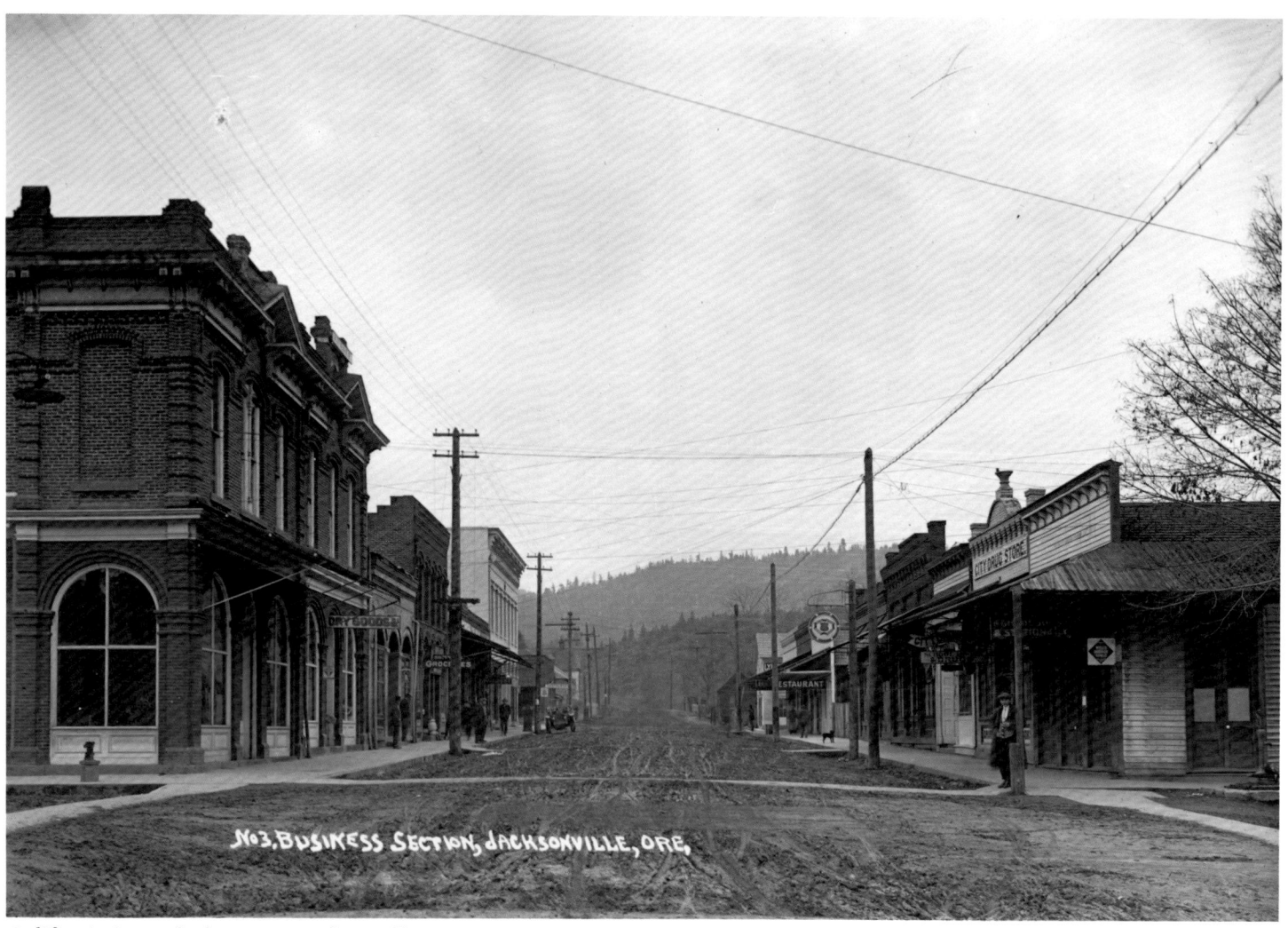

California Street, looking west, Jacksonville, ca. 1910 (OHS Neg. OrHi 15955)

Jacksonville 1910-1994

Despite its rapidly fading prominence and wealth after the turn of the century, Jacksonville remained an important city and the seat of Jackson County. In 1905 the Rogue River Power Company built a transformer station at the western edge of the commercial core. California Street was soon festooned with wires for telephone and electric service; the appointments of every modern and successful commercial district of the early twentieth century. As this photo shows, Jacksonville's old buildings were nestled beneath a veritable spider's web of overhead cabling.

Throughout the mining period, and even into this century, the roadbed of California Street was little more than a quagmire. Sticky mud in the spring and winter gave way to a dusty path in the summer. Merchants often paid the cost of stone or brick pathways that allowed their patrons to cross the street without ruining their clothes. Such improvements were proud elements on many Main Streets.

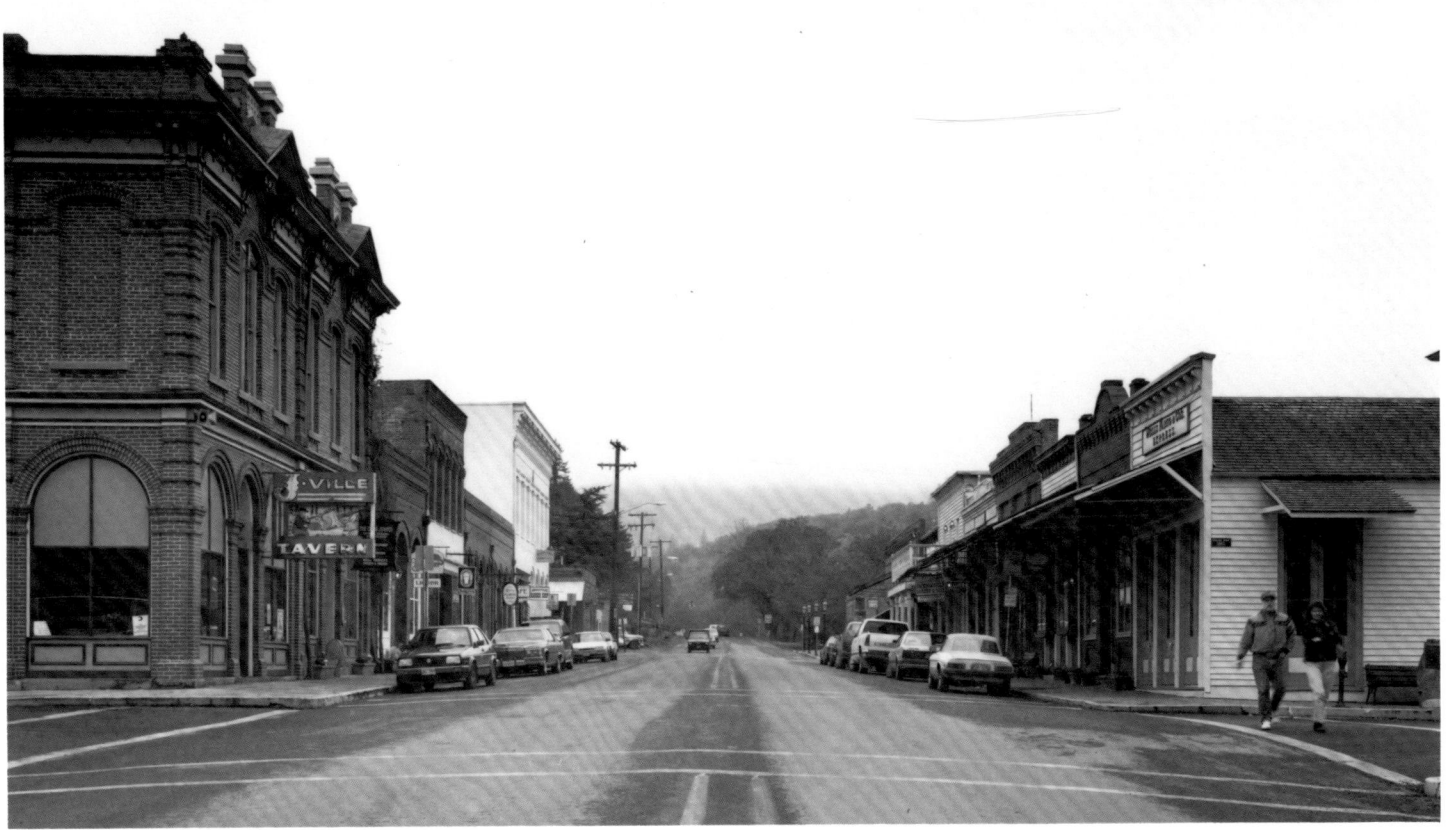

California Street, looking east, Jacksonville, 1994 (OHS Neg. Lot 824-26)

History has been kind to Jacksonville's buildings, inoculating them from much of the change and remodeling that have so altered other communities. Today, to a far greater extent that most cities, Jacksonville's main street retains a high degree of visual consistency with its historic period. But Jacksonville's success, much of it the result of preservation and the effort to keep Jacksonville as it was has also mandated, certain improvements on the past. Those aspects of main street that don't mesh with modern sensibilities or economic practicality in a "restored" townscape are discarded, no matter how authentic. So, in Jacksonville, the muddy streets have given way to modern asphalt, traversed by painted crosswalks in place of the masonry paths. Overhead, most of the spider's web of wires have been buried, returning the sky to the pre-modern era while still providing for the creature comforts of the modern community.

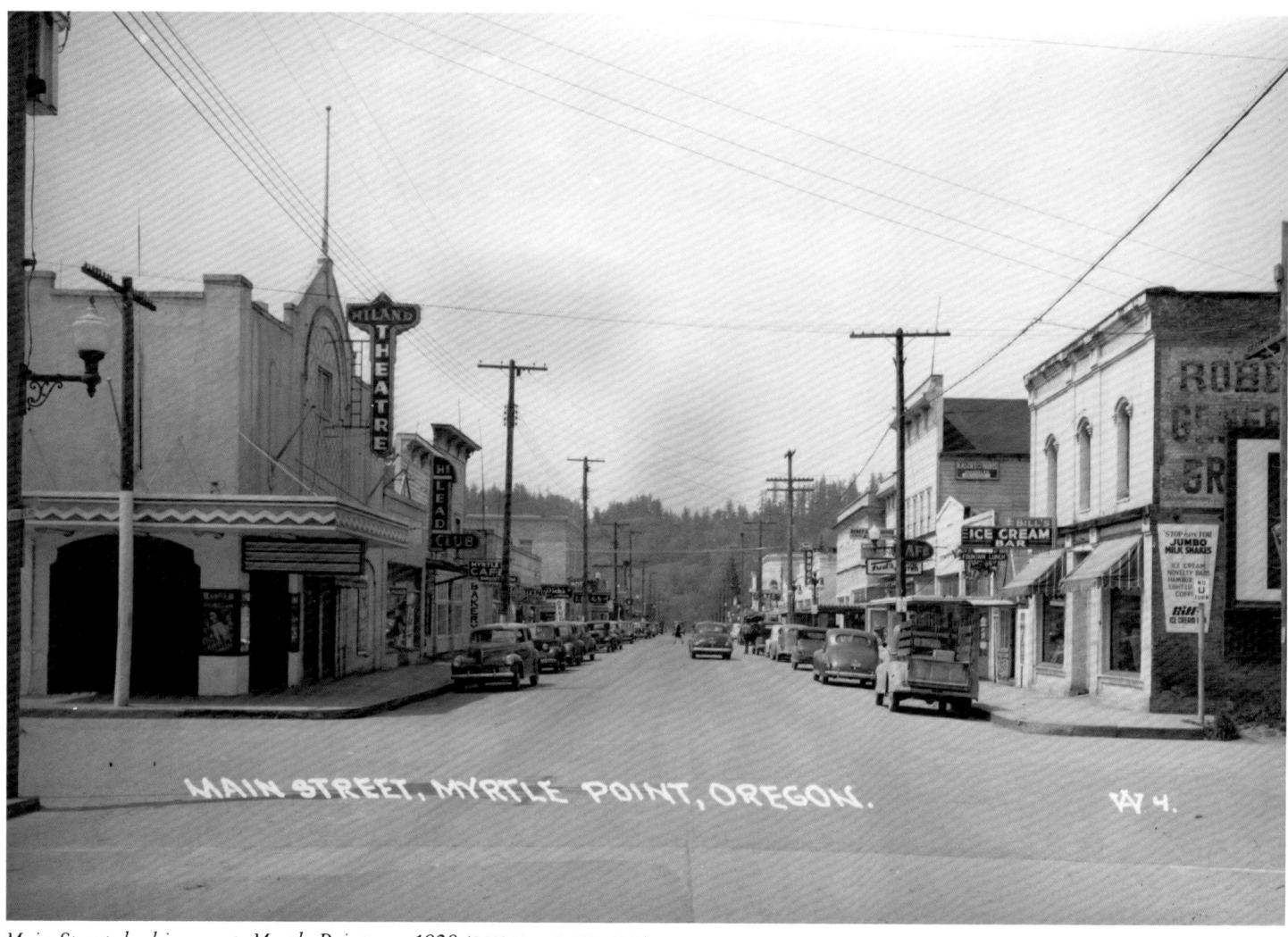

Main Street, looking west, Myrtle Point, ca. 1928 (OHS Neg. OrHi 16547)

Myrtle Point 1928-1994

The main street of any community was once roughly analogous to its "company" face. Main Street was not only the internal focus of social and economic life, it was the most tangible expression of a community to the greater world; a visible icon of a city's prosperity and an advertisement for potential investment. In southwestern Oregon, many smaller communities lacked the financial resources to compete with the big city, be it Roseburg, Medford, or Eugene. Early merchants here and elsewhere accordingly adopted the so-called false-front style for their wood-frame buildings. Simple single-story gable roof volumes were hidden behind elaborately detailed two-story facades that imitated the brick commercial blocks of larger and more prosperous communities. Often, as a city grew and gained in prosperity, false-fronts were actually replaced with the brick or concrete buildings they imitated. Other times, when the local economy failed to justify such an investment, false-fronts endured well past their builder's expectations or hopes.

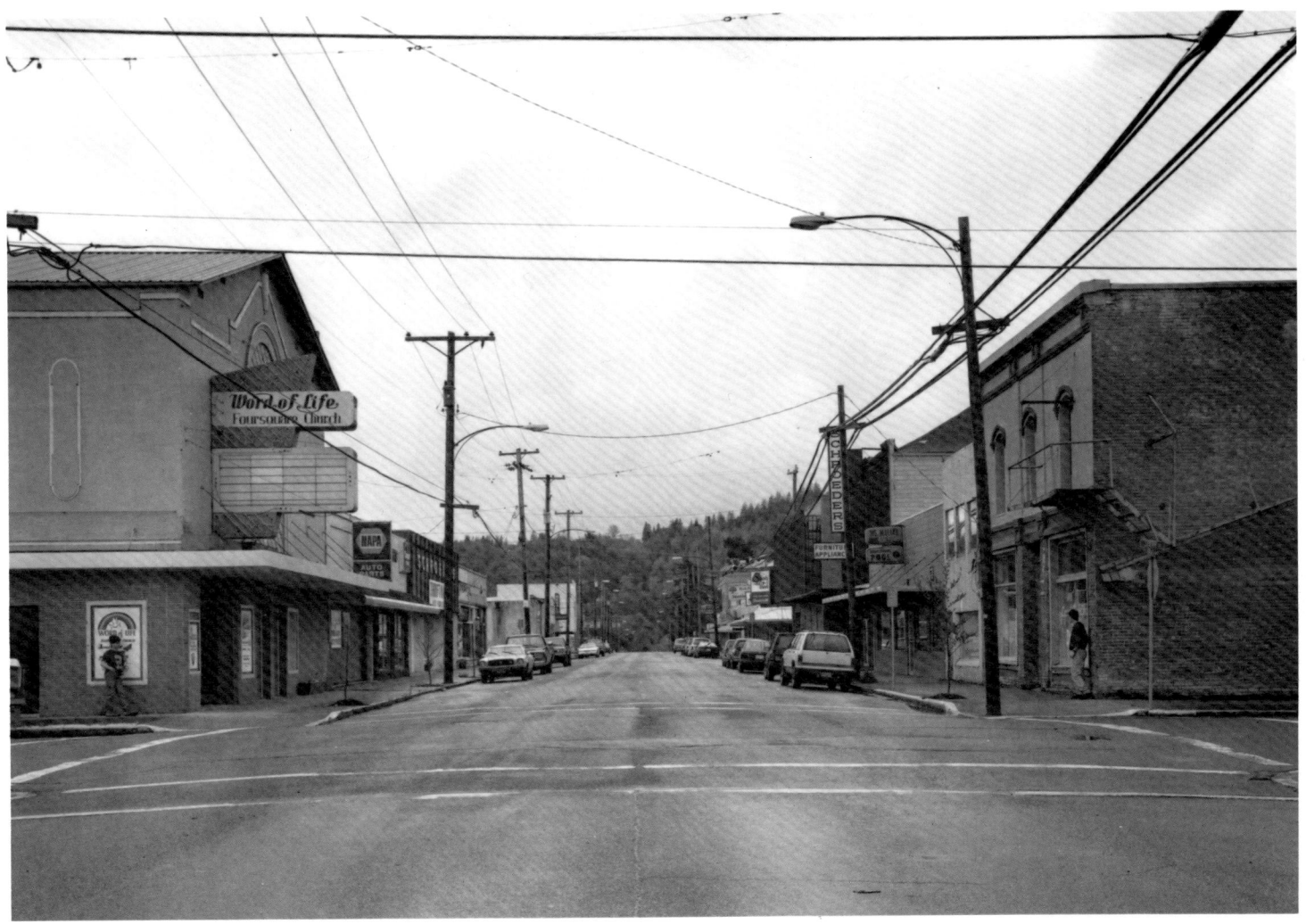

Main Street, looking west, Myrtle Point, 1994 (OHS Neg. Lot 824-28)

Myrtle Point was incorporated in 1887, with an economy based on the surrounding timber stands and agriculture. Well positioned on the Coquille River, and later the highway, the town was as hopeful of development as most other small communities in southwestern Oregon. But as the historic view shows, well into the 1930s no boom in Myrtle Point had led to the wholesale replacement of its early wood-frame buildings. Even today, some of these original wood structures still survive, such as the building that houses Schroder's Furniture, on the right. The two falsefronts that once stood opposite this structure have given way to smaller scale buildings. These modest, functional, buildings, date from an era in which developers apparently had little or no pretense about the role of architecture in Myrtle Point's future.

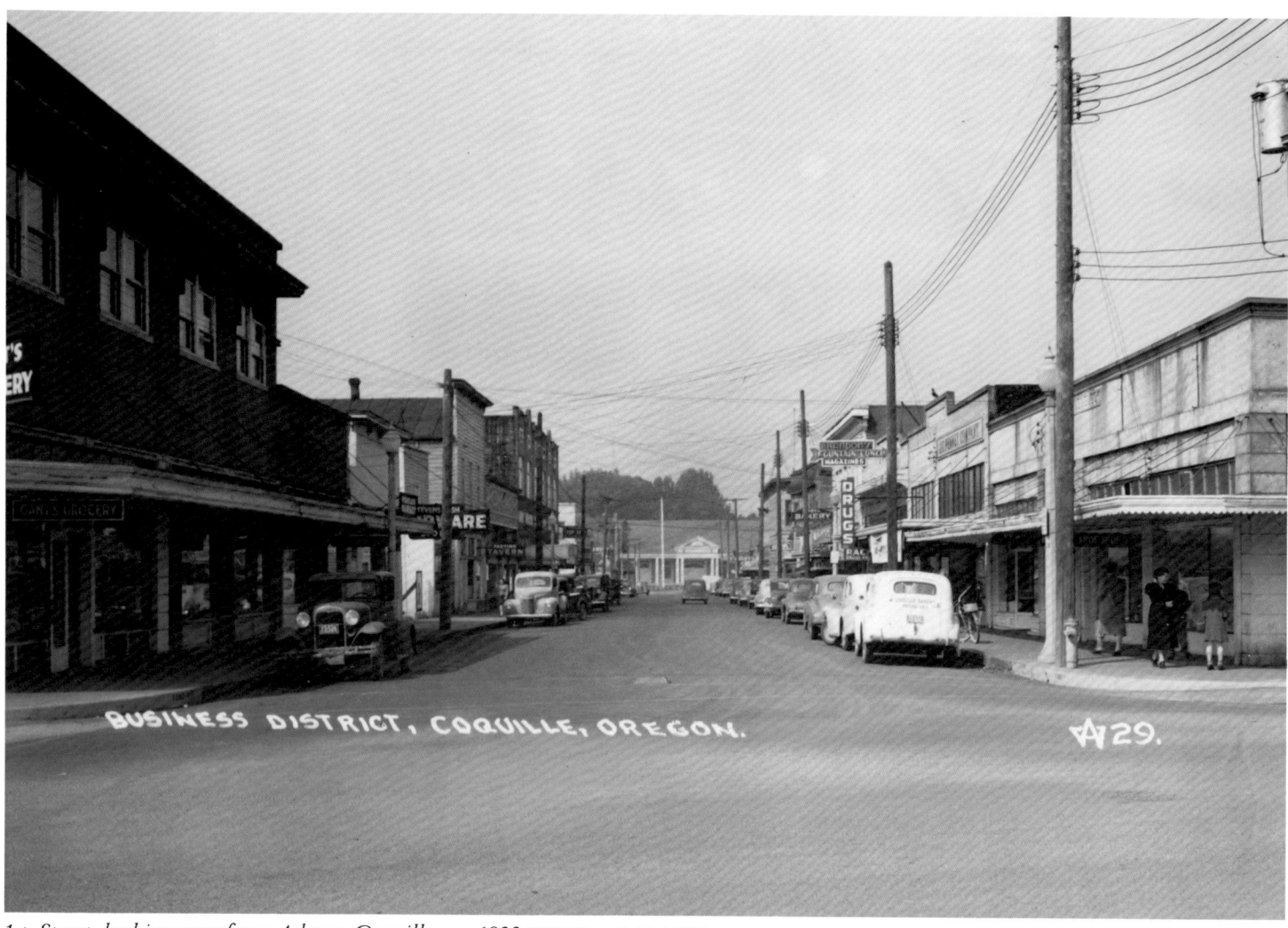

1st Street, looking west from Adams, Coquille, ca. 1932 (OHS Neg. OrHi 14897)

Coquille 1932-1994

Located on the Coquille River, later served by both rail and highway, Coquille grew into a major transportation center in Coos County. Incorporated in 1885, the Coos County seat was moved to the growing city from Empire in 1896. Coquille's first main street faced the waterfront. When the railroad replaced the river as the primary shipping point, the depot was built along the waterfront and Main Street remained facing the depot. Later, with the rise of the automobile and the construction of State Highway 42, Coquille's main street migrated west, to Adams, along that newly important transportation corridor. Ongoing construction in the prosperous timber community reflected its stable economy and promising future.

In Coquille, as in many cities, fire plays a huge role in the history of main street. Coquille's first major blaze was in 1892, destroying almost 75 percent of the commercial core. The St. Patrick's day fire of 1918 again swept much of the area and

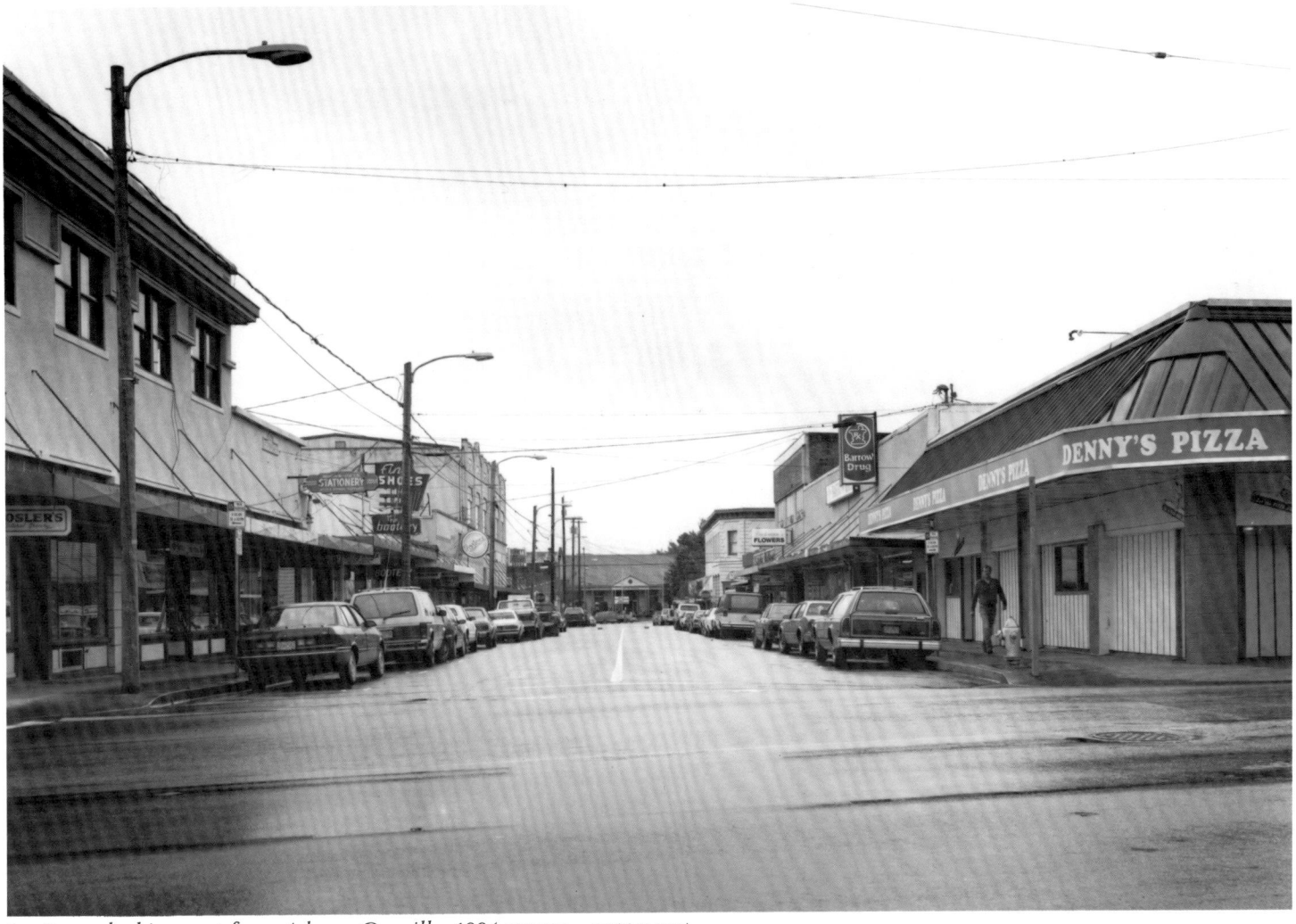

1st Street, looking west from Adams, Coquille, 1994 (OHS Neg. LOT 824-29)

most of the present buildings were constructed in its aftermath. As the historic view reveals, by the 1930s 1st Street had developed into a fairly regular streetscape of modest concrete and brick structures with simple lines; a pedestrian-friendly core visually terminated by the public library building.

Today, sixty years later, most of 1930 Coquille's buildings still stand. Some, like the Nosler Building (1924), on the right, are fairly intact. Others, like the Shelley Block, on the left, are not. In 1937 this building housed three small businesses facing 1st Street, with a cafe to the rear. Today its lone occupant, a local pizzeria, is hidden beneath a Darth Vader-like awning that may result from some unconscious attempt to copy the mansard roof of a certain national fast food franchise — a design obviously "McInappropriate" on Main Street.

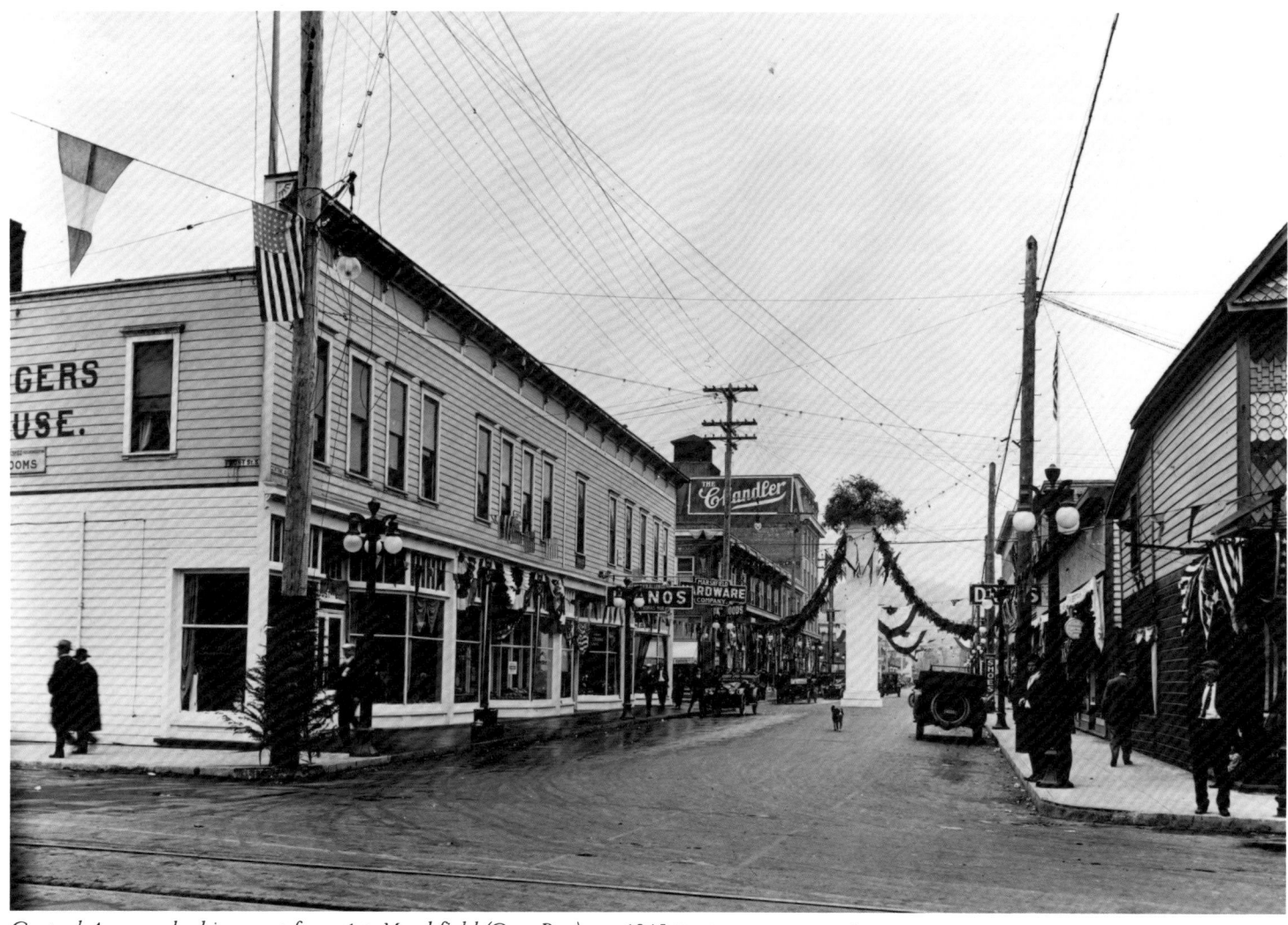

Central Avenue, looking west from 1st, Marshfield (Coos Bay), ca. 1915 (OHS Neg. OrHi 90528)

Coos Bay 1915-1994

Known as Marshfield until the end of 1944, the City of Coos Bay grew around the natural feature from which it later took its name. First founded in the 1860s, by 1898 one historian described the city as "the business center for the coal mines, farming districts and logging camps" of Coos County. Built in 1908, the impressive six-story Chandler Hotel dominates the downtown skyline. This modern, fireproof accommodation succeeded the wood-frame Rogers House, shown on the corner, as the city's prime hostelry. The 1922 Front Street fire proved the wisdom of fireproof construction. The Rogers House was razed in that fire's aftermath and replaced with the present Hub Building, itself now listed on the National Register, as is the Chandler.

But it is not just the buildings that are remarkable in these views. What is most striking is the exuberance, the activity, of the historic photograph. Cars, pedestrians, even dogs, were all drawn to Central Avenue, evidence of the vital and lively role the street once played in this community. Nor was Central unusual. In the days before television, national holidays or local events were often a time of festive public

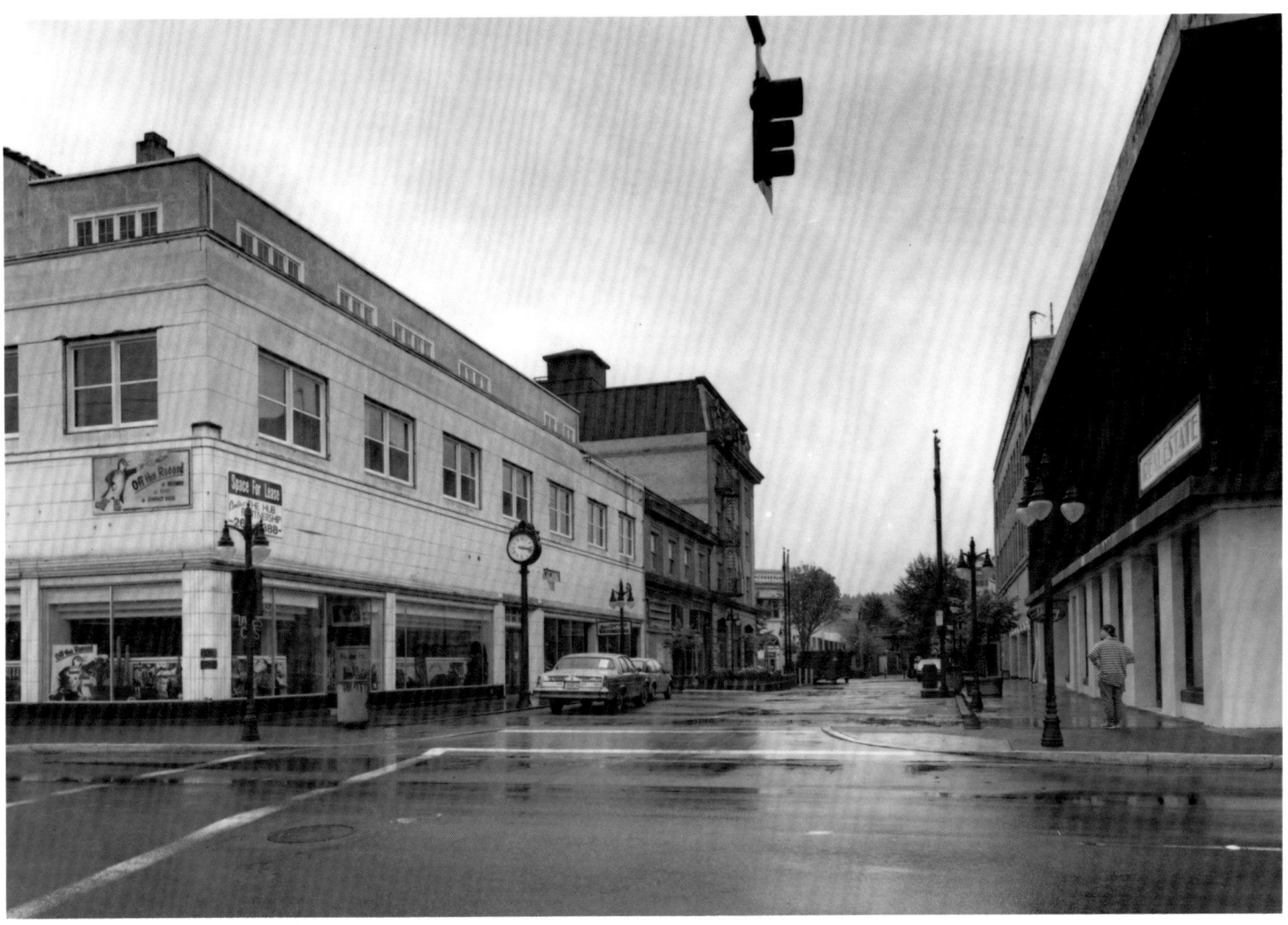

Central Avenue, looking west from 1st, Coos Bay, 1994 (OHS Neg. Lot 824-27)

celebrations. Main Street was often host to a parade or marching band and its buildings and streetlights were bedecked with all sorts of decorations to mark the event. Here, garlands, banners, and flags help us identify the holiday as a patriotic one, either the Fourth of July, Memorial Day, or, most likely, what was then known as Armistice Day.

All too often, the vitality of Main Street waned in the years after World War II. Many traditional retail areas struggled against new competition, particularly the ubiquitous mall. Facing this new threat, some Main Streets were transformed into new visages. Cross-streets were closed off, historic buildings were cloistered behind modern materials, even covered walkways and piped-in music were added in generally misguided attempts to make Main Street more mall-like. Unfortunately, the "malling" of Main Street was only rarely successful. In recent years Coos Bay has begun removing the remnants of one such an effort, slowly reclaiming and revitalizing Mall Block 1, as this stretch of Coos Bay's main street had been christened.

EASTERN OREGON

Dr. Ward Tonsfeldt

Hood River *Baker City* *Bend*

The Dalles *Ontario* *Klamath Falls*

Pendleton *Prairie City* *Lakeview*

La Grande *John Day*

The two-thirds of Oregon that lie east of the Cascade Mountains have a different geography and a different culture than the western part of the state. Immediately east of the Cascades, the long valley of the Deschutes runs north to the Columbia River. To the south, the Klamath Basin slopes toward California. East of the Deschutes country is the John Day Valley and the Blue Mountains, and farther east, the Wallowas and the Snake River. In the southeast corner of Oregon the geographical pattern of basin and range extends through Lake, Harney, and Malheur counties. The northeastern corner offers the Columbia Plateau and the rich wheat lands of Morrow, Gilliam, and Umatilla counties.

For the towns east of the Cascades, geography is fate. The high altitude, short growing season, and limited water have made farming impossible in all but a few favored locations. As a result, nineteenth century settlement was sparse and the population density remains low. Communities throughout the region are separated by miles of open land. History has tied these towns and people to natural resource industries. The vicissitudes of mining, ranching, and timber have shaped the region.

Far more eastern Oregon communities have failed than flourished. In 1910, for example, there were perhaps 5,000 people living in the small towns served by the Sumpter Valley Railroad; today there are scarcely 500.

The towns in the following photographs are the survivors. Each has a different story, but they have in common the vigor and tenacity of their citizens and the regional heritage of life "east of the mountains."

Dr. Ward Tonsfeldt, Professor of Humanities at Central Oregon Community College, currently serves as Vice-Chair for the State Advisory Committee for Historic Preservation.

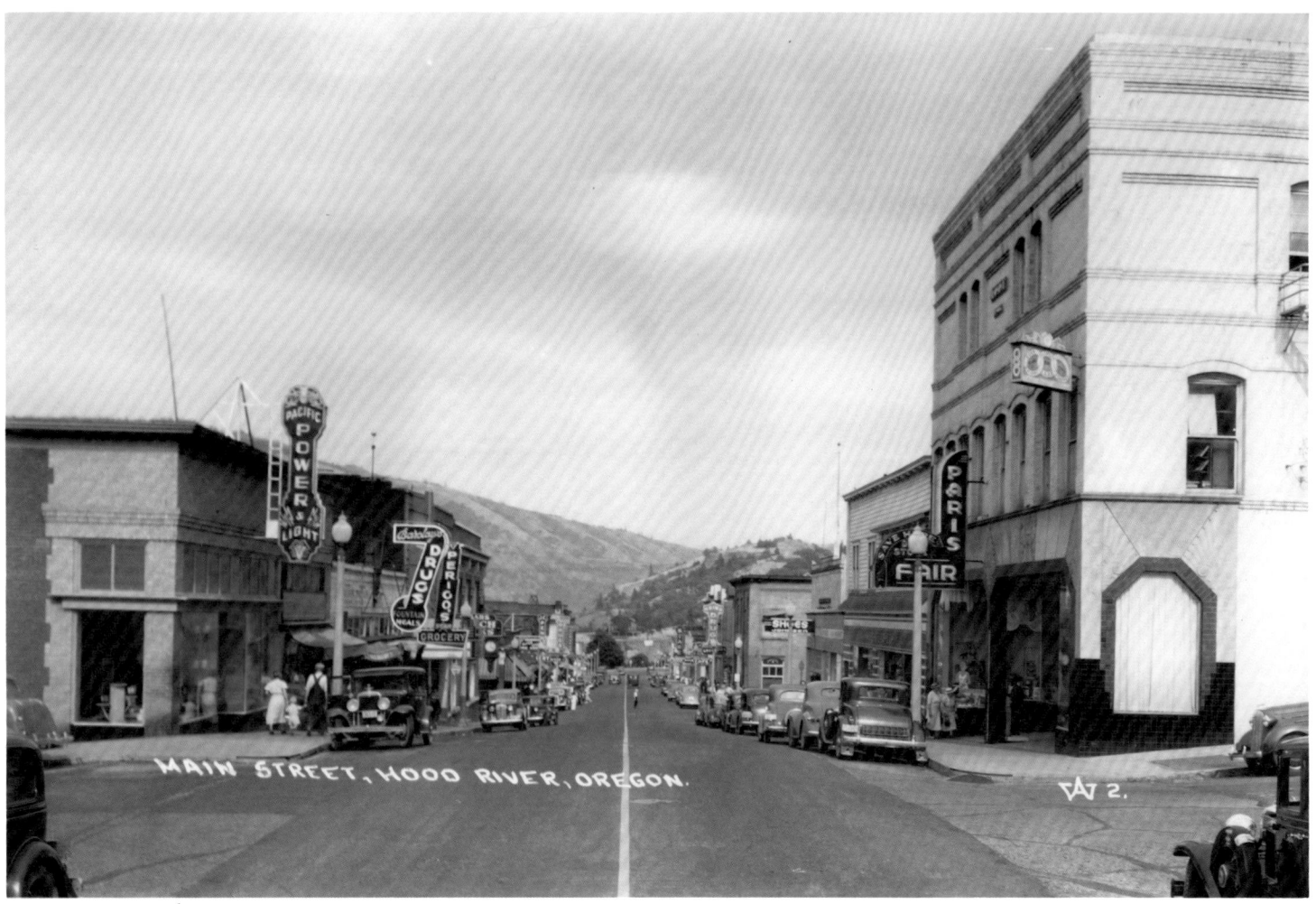

Main Street, Hood River, ca. 1930 (OHS Neg. OrHi 15869)

Hood River 1930-1994

Euro-American settlement at Hood River began in 1854, when Nathan and Mary Coe started a farm near the mount of the river. The Coes marketed their produce - fruit, vegetables, and beef - in The Dalles, thus beginning in a small way the agricultural tradition of the Hood River Valley.

Hood River grew up as a port on the Columbia, offering goods and services to the settlers on both sides of the river. The wheat and salmon industries provided additional trade in the 1870s and early 1880s, and then in 1882 the railroad reached Hood River on its path across the continent. The lumber industry followed the railroad, and by the turn of the century Hood River had farming, fishing, transportation, and lumber on its list of assets.

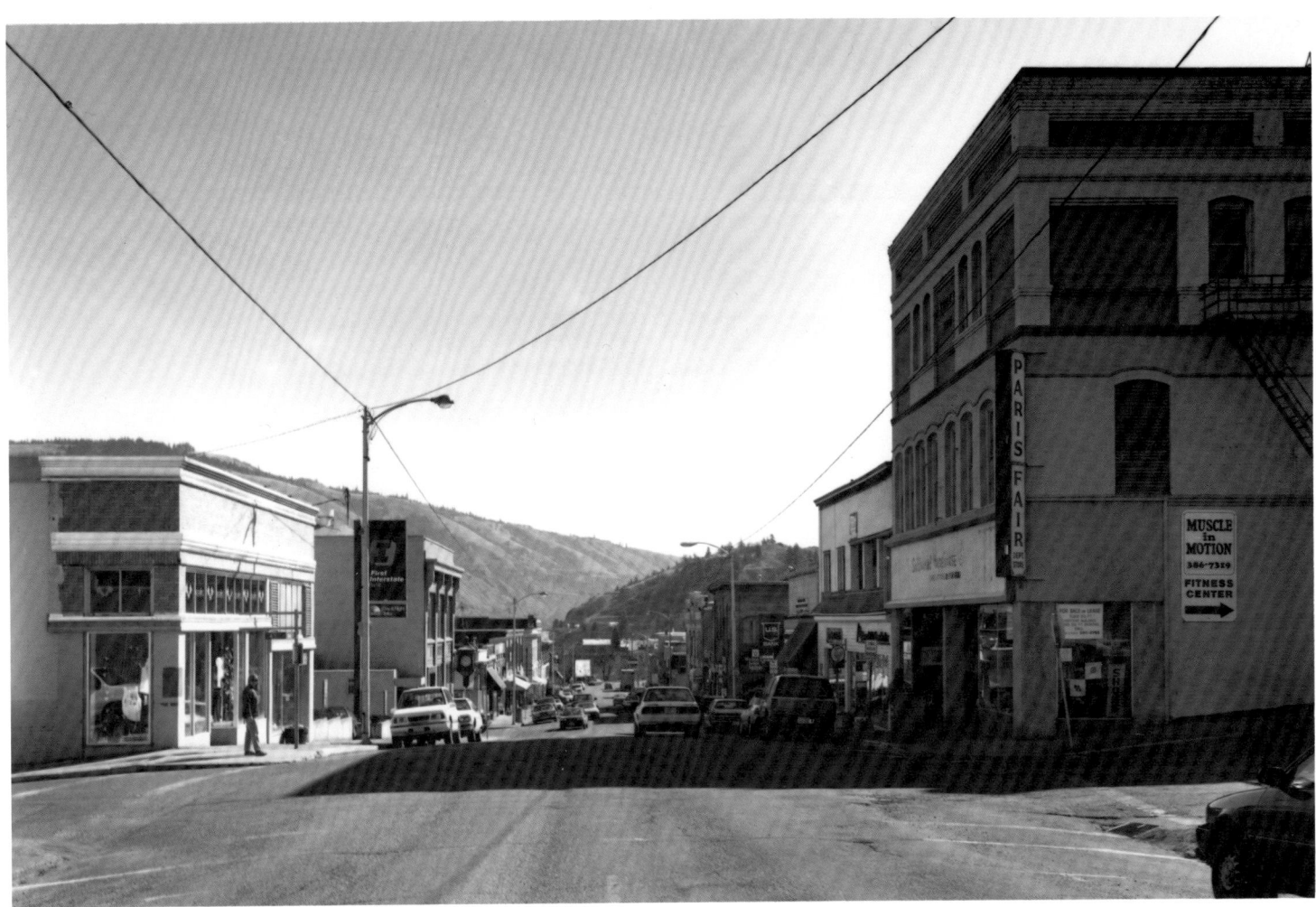

Main Street, Hood River, 1994 (OHS Neg. Lot 824-30)

This mix made for a stable and prosperous community. The historic view of Fourth and Oak streets, taken in the middle 1930s, shows solid storefronts, tidy cars, and well dressed shoppers. Perhaps the most noteworthy feature of the street scene, however, is the array of neon signs set to beckon evening customers. Sixty years later Hood River's Main Street has changed very little. The distinctive signs are gone, thanks to a city ordinance, but the landmark buildings remain. The Paris Fair/Odd Fellows Hall has had several facades since it was built in 1906. It is now on the National Register and is being restored. Next to it is the Paris Fair annex, which is the only frame building visible in the historic photo, and remains the single wooden commercial building on Hood River's Main Street.

The Dalles 1930-1994

The Dalles, which is the oldest Euro-American settlement east of the mountains, is located near sites occupied by Native Americans for several centuries. White settlement of The Dalles began with the Wascopam Mission in 1838. The next decade saw The Dalles grow as Oregon Trail parties stopped there to put their wagons onto rafts for the final leg of the journey down the Columbia River to Portland and Oregon City. In the 1850s and 1860s the military establishment at Fort Dalles contributed to the settlement. Wasco County and Dalles City were formed by the Territorial Legislature in 1854 and 1855. During the gold rush of the 1860s, the city served thousands of hopeful prospectors traveling upriver to the gold fields of Oregon, Washington, and Idaho. The gold fever waned in the 1870s and 1880s, but The Dalles recovered with the river trade, then the railroad, bringing additional commerce.

By the turn of the century, The Dalles had transformed itself from a frontier boomtown to a commercial center for the Columbia Plateau. New industries including fruit packing and shipping, wool processing, and salmon canning provided jobs and opportunities.

The historic photo of a street scene in the 1930s features the Odd Fellows building, which remains a landmark of the downtown commercial historic district. Built in 1904 of brick, with elaborate corbelling and quoining, and a sheet metal cornice, the building offered the usual combination of a lodge hall upstairs and retail space on the ground floor. Lodges like the International Order of Odd Fellows, or the Knights of Pythias, were an important element of small town life. They provided social services for their members, opportunities for bonding, and - in a time before E-mail or FAX - the best communication network available.

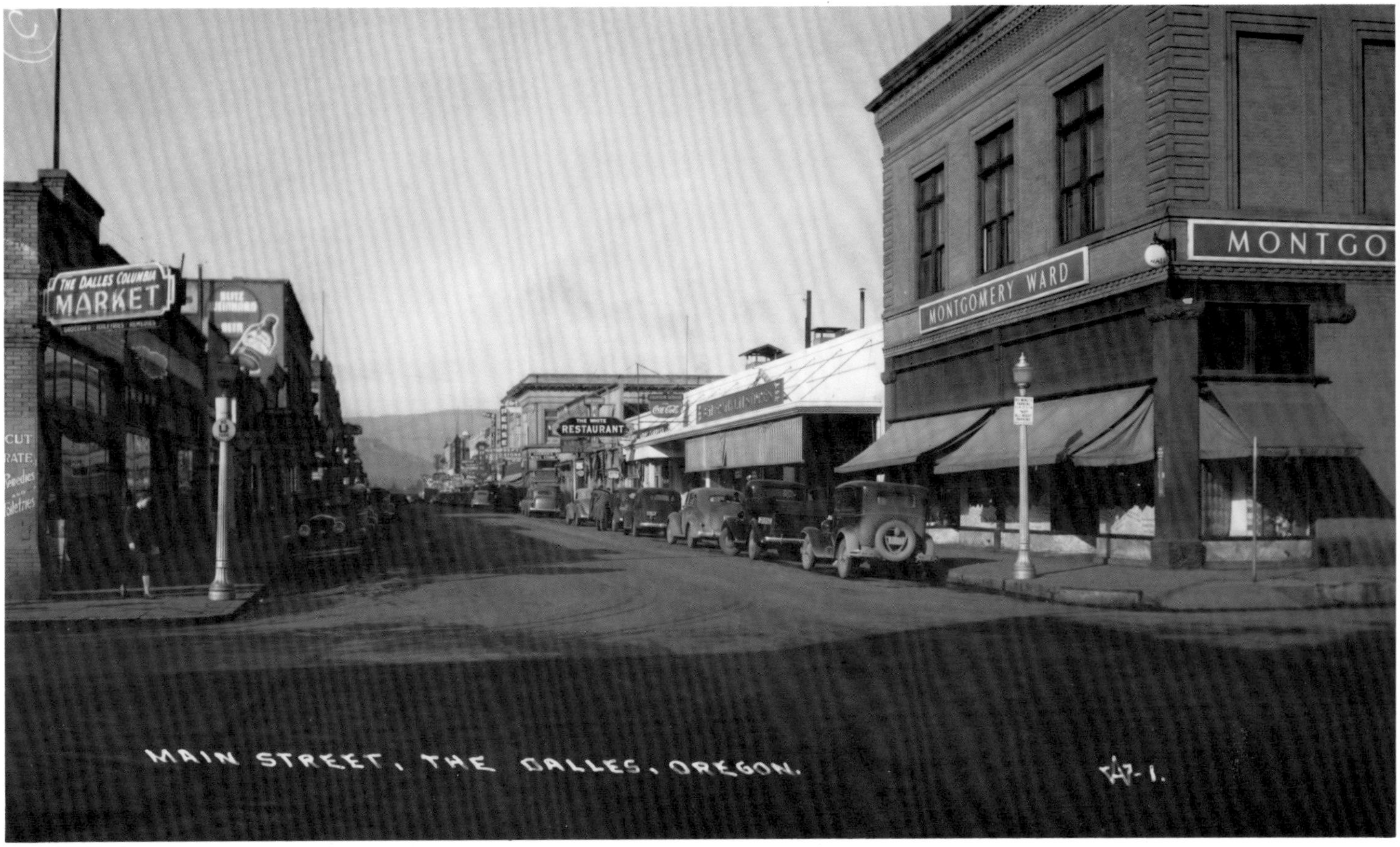

East 2nd Street, looking west from Laughlin, The Dalles, ca 1930 (OHS Neg. OrHi 15094)

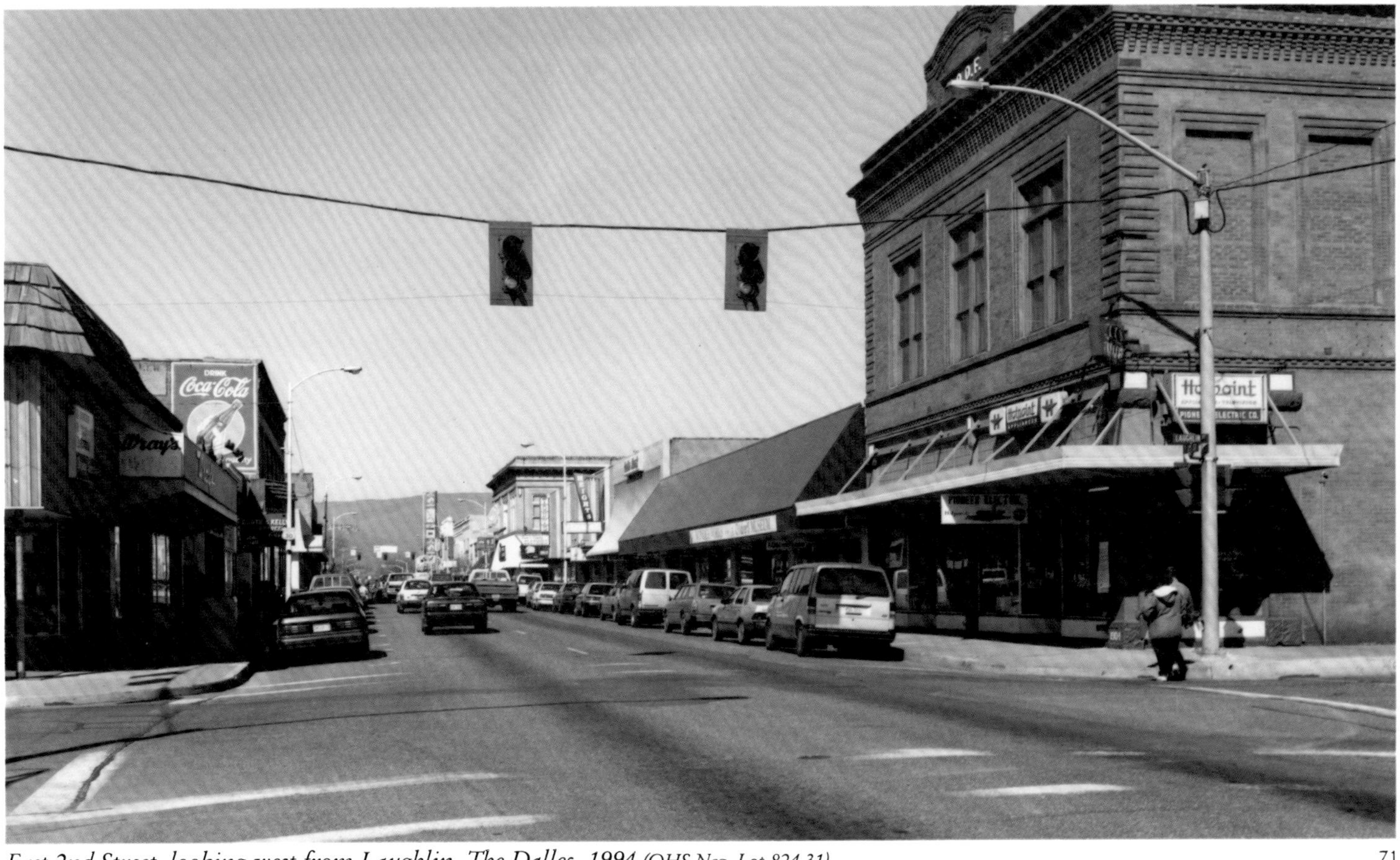

East 2nd Street, looking west from Laughlin, The Dalles, 1994 (OHS Neg. Lot 824-31)

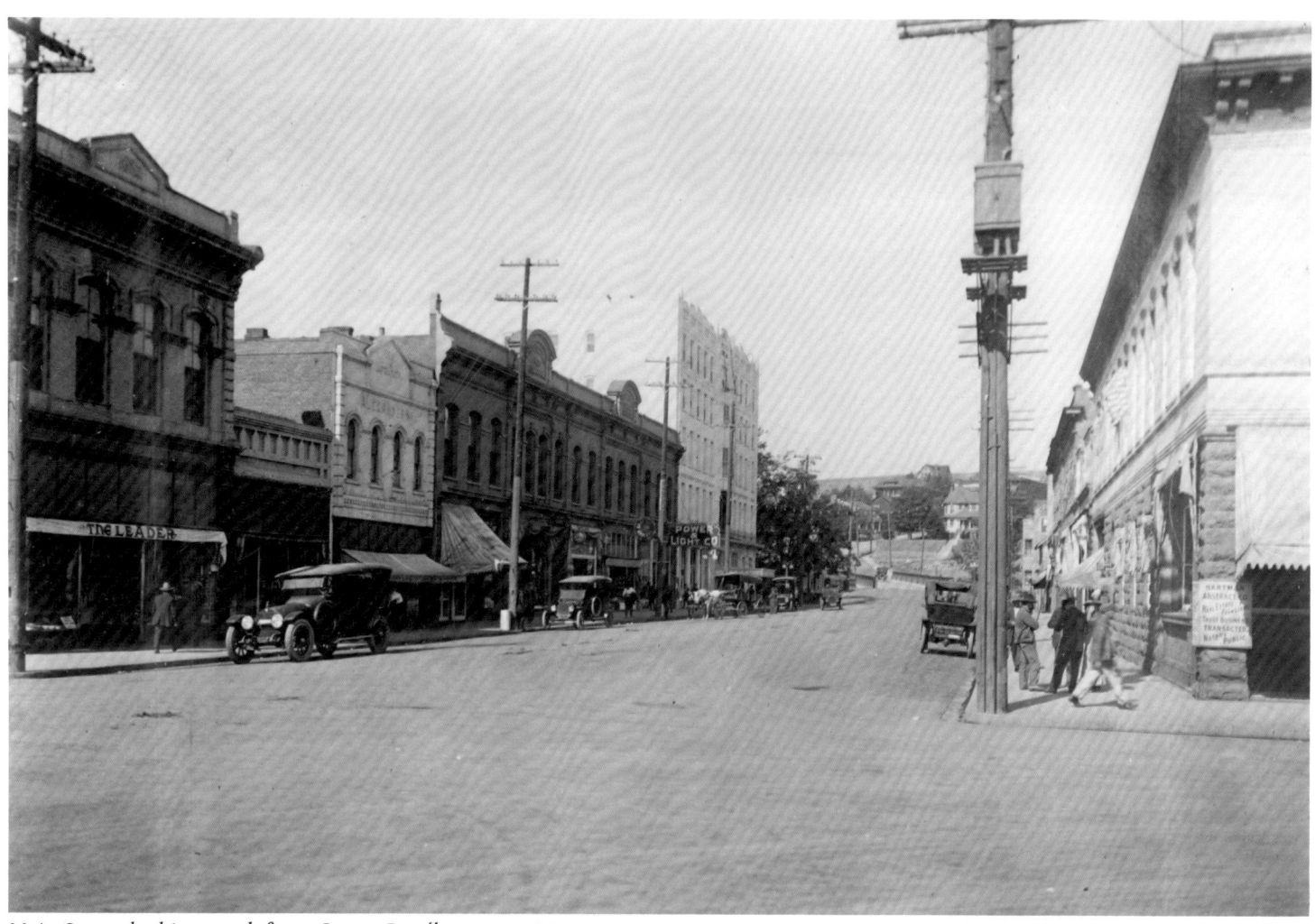

Main Street, looking north from Court, Pendleton, ca. 1920 (OHS Neg. OrHi 086095)

Pendleton 1920–1994

Since its incorporation in 1880, Pendleton has been the dominant town in northeastern Oregon's wheat country. A series of floods and fires challenged the town during the 1880s and 1890s, but brick buildings, levees, and the citizens' persistence finally won out. Pendleton entered the twentieth century as a producer of flour and wool. In the World War I years, demand and prices for these two commodities reached record levels. As a result, Pendleton enjoyed prosperity and sophistication that were the envy of other eastern Oregon towns.

The historic photo shows Pendleton's Main Street in the early 1920s. The five-story building of light colored masonry in the center of the photo is the Hotel Pendleton. It

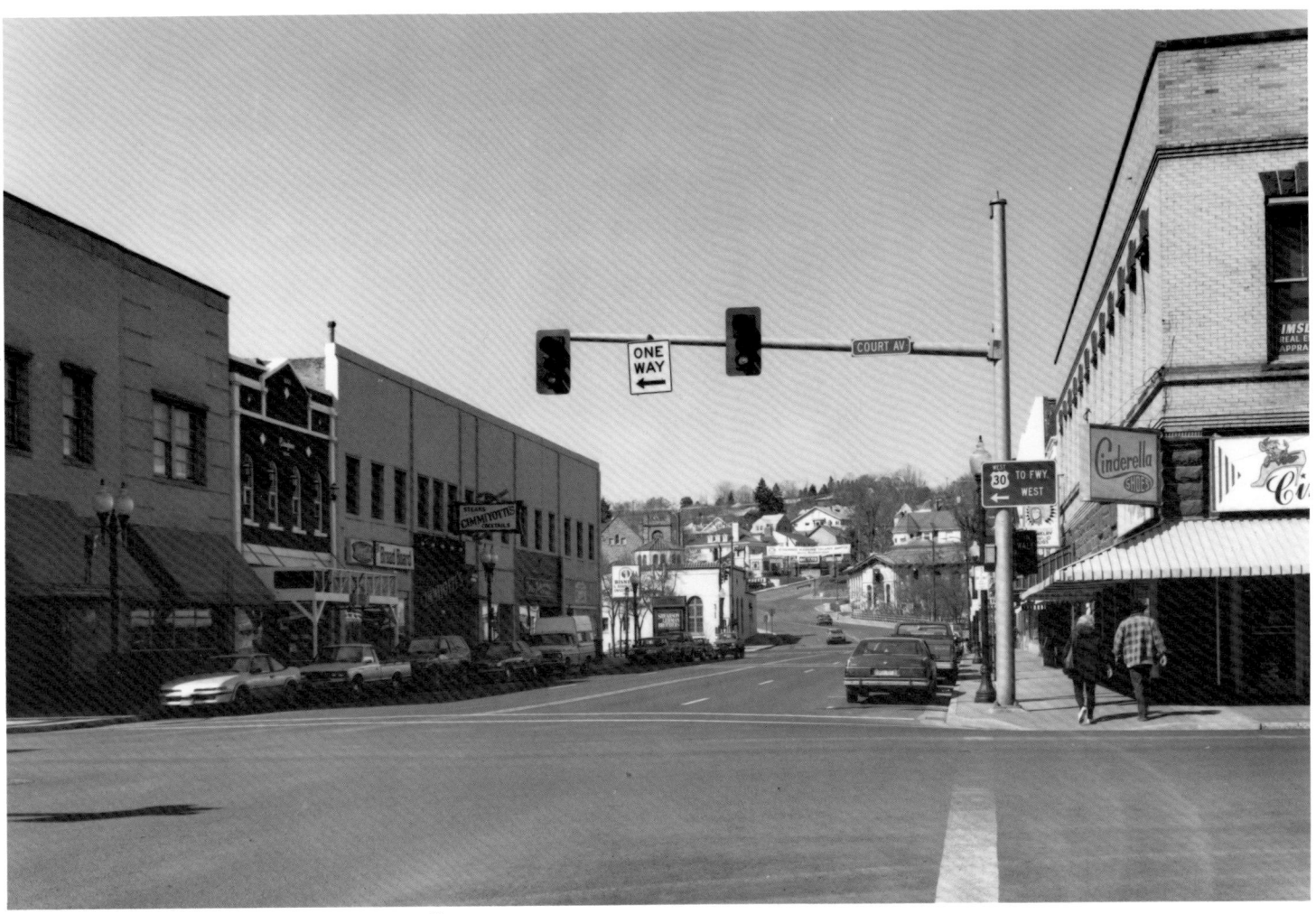

Main Street, looking north from Court, Pendleton, 1994 (OHS Neg. Lot 824-32)

began as a two-story frame structure in the 1870s. In 1888 it was replaced by a masonry building that grew to five stories in 1914. Downtown hotels like the Pendleton could not compete with motels in the 1950s and 1960s, however, and the building was razed in 1964. A more subtle process has changed the other buildings. The original structures on both sides of Main had ornamental crests on their parapets, corbelling, and projecting cornices. These details have been removed from all but the Alexander's Dry Goods building, located on the left side of the street near the center of the block.

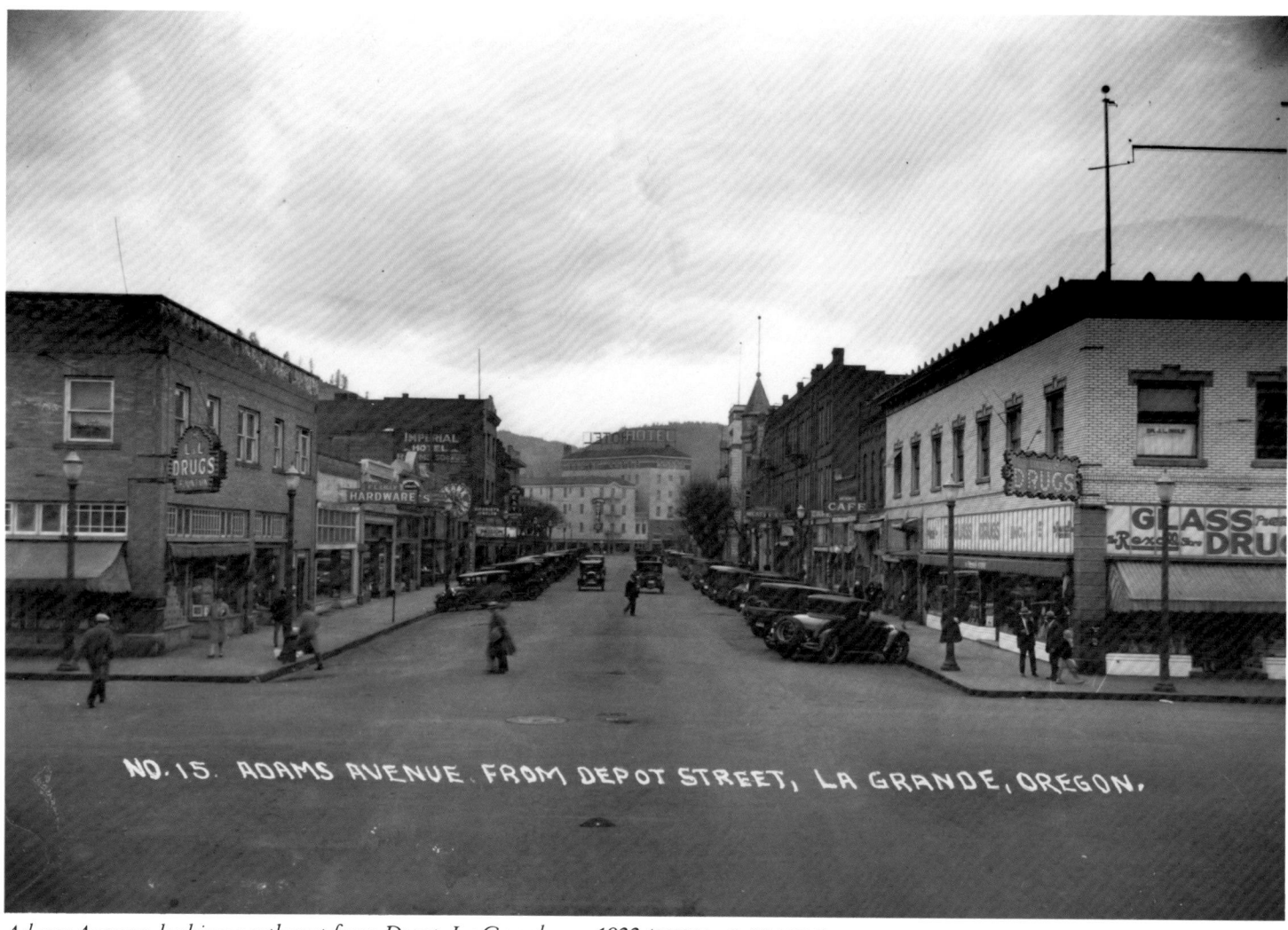

Adams Avenue, looking northwest from Depot, La Grande, ca. 1922 (OHS Neg.OrHi 16139)

La Grande 1922-1994

In the spring of 1862 Benjamin and Fannie Brown settled in the Grand Ronde Valley near the Oregon Trail. When gold was discovered in the Blue Mountains a year later, the Browns found themselves strategically located on the route to the gold camps. They built a hotel, and the village of Browntown slowly grew up around it. In the next decade Browntown became La Grande.

In 1884, the transcontinental railroad was approaching La Grande, but the original route would have missed the town, eclipsing its chances for future growth. A local businessman, Daniel Chapin, donated land to the Oregon Railway and Navigation Company and persuaded the company to alter its route.   La Grande became the division point for the railroad, and the site of the railroad maintenance shop complex,

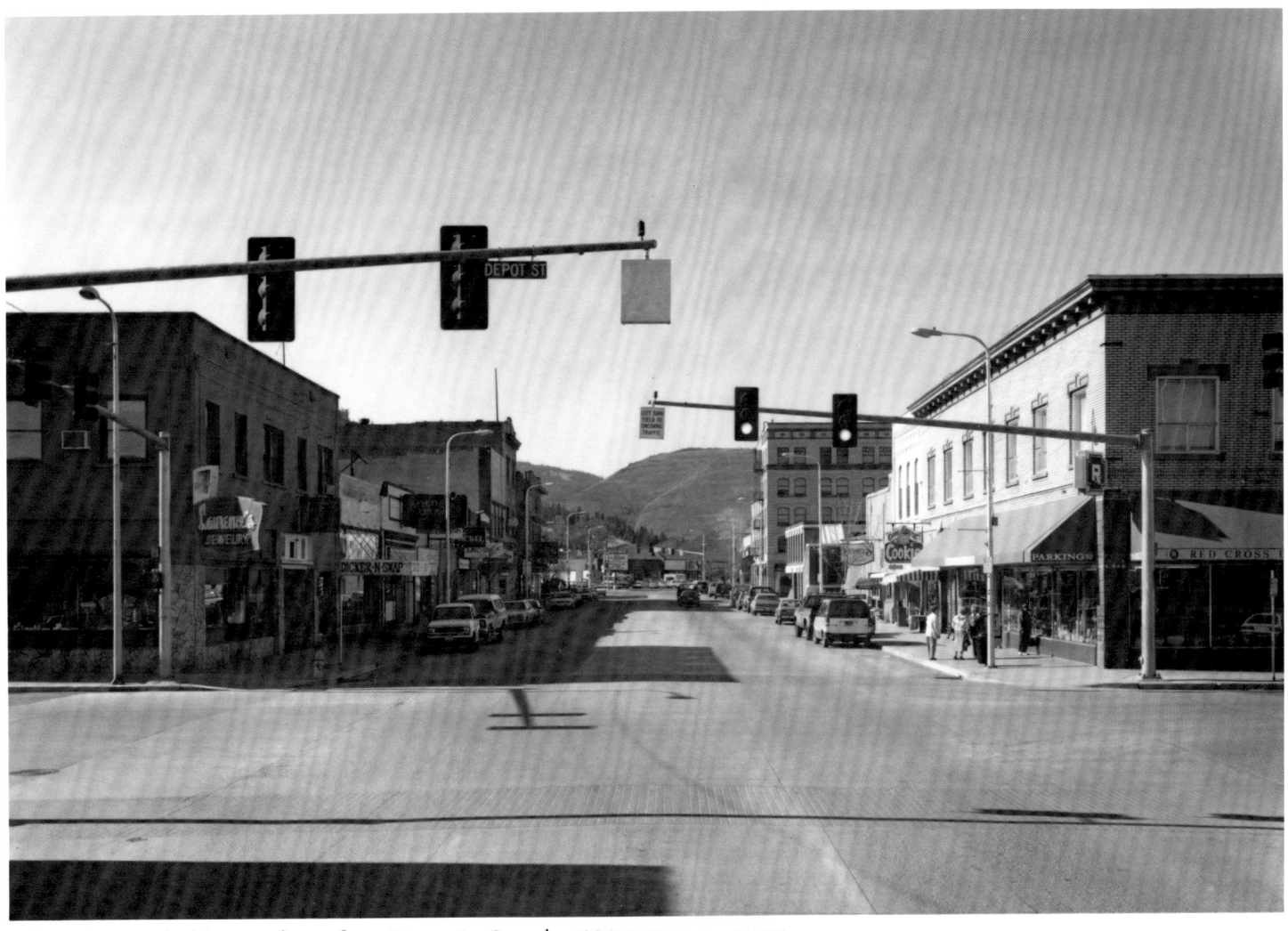

Adams Avenue, looking northwest from Depot, La Grande, 1994 (OHS Neg.Lot 824-33)

which was soon the town's largest employer. Industries following the railroad included two substantial lumber mills--Bowman Hicks and Mt. Emily--and a sugar beet refinery.

The historic view of Adams Avenue from Depot Street shows La Grande at the height of its career as a railroad and industrial center. The imposing La Grande Hotel at the end of Adams Street was build in 1926 and survived only until 1942. Its rival, the Sacajawea Hotel, fared somewhat better but succumbed to the wreckers in 1970. Although these landmark structures are gone, the brick buildings that line the main streets remain, setting the character of this eastern Oregon community.

Baker City 1890-1994

In 1861 prospector Henry Griffin struck gold on the Powder River in the Blue Mountains. During the following year, thousands of miners crowded into the area, building the town of Auburn, Oregon's version of the roaring camps of the Sierras. Auburn proved ephemeral, but its nearby rival, Baker City, endured after the placer claims were exhausted and the miners moved on to new bonanzas.

Baker City grew slowly during the 1860s and 1870s, beginning with a few houses, a blacksmith shop, a boarding house, a quartz mill and, of course, a saloon. By 1870, the town was the seat of Baker County and had its own newspaper. During these years, the town developed as a trading center for the ranches and mines of the Blue Mountains. Then in 1884, the transcontinental railroad reached Baker City, connecting it to the outside world and assuring its future. The Oregon Lumber Company built a large mill in the center of town, merchants built solid stone storefronts, and Baker City emerged as Eastern Oregon's first metropolis.

At the turn of the century, Baker City's Warshauer-Geiser Grand Hotel, was reputedly the finest hostelry east of the Cascades. The hotel's Italianate tower, visible in the right foreground of the historic photo, punctuated the east side of Main Street. Directly across from the Grand and built in the same year, 1889, is the Heilner Building. Founded by pioneer merchant S. A. Heilner in 1873, the business still flourishes in the same location. Today, the Grand is shorn of its tower, and the Heilner Building has lost its third story. Thanks to civic pride and a thoughtful restoration program, however, Baker City retains a great deal of its character and frontier charm.

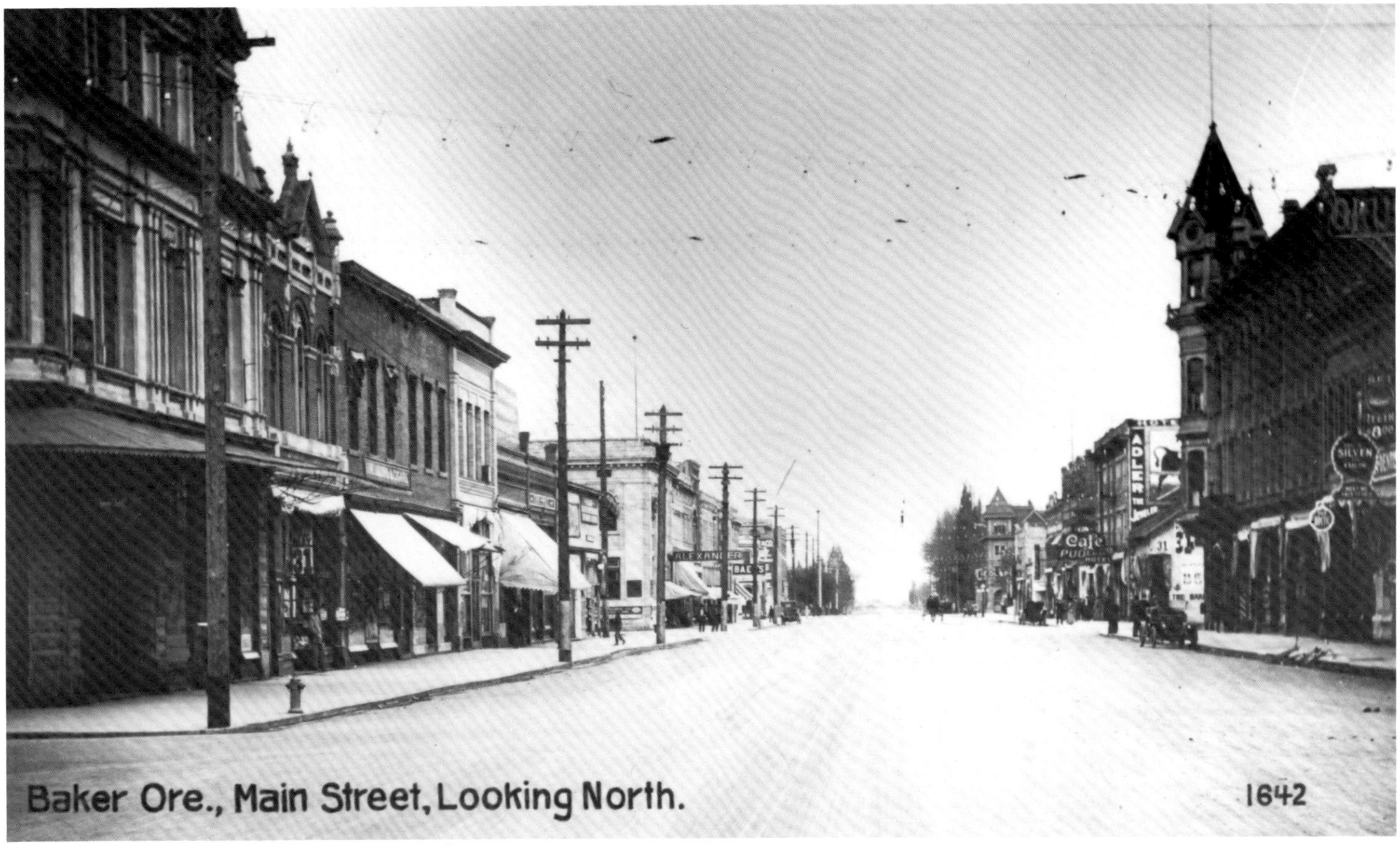

Main Street, looking north from Court, Baker City, ca. 1890 (OHS Neg. OrHi 51974)

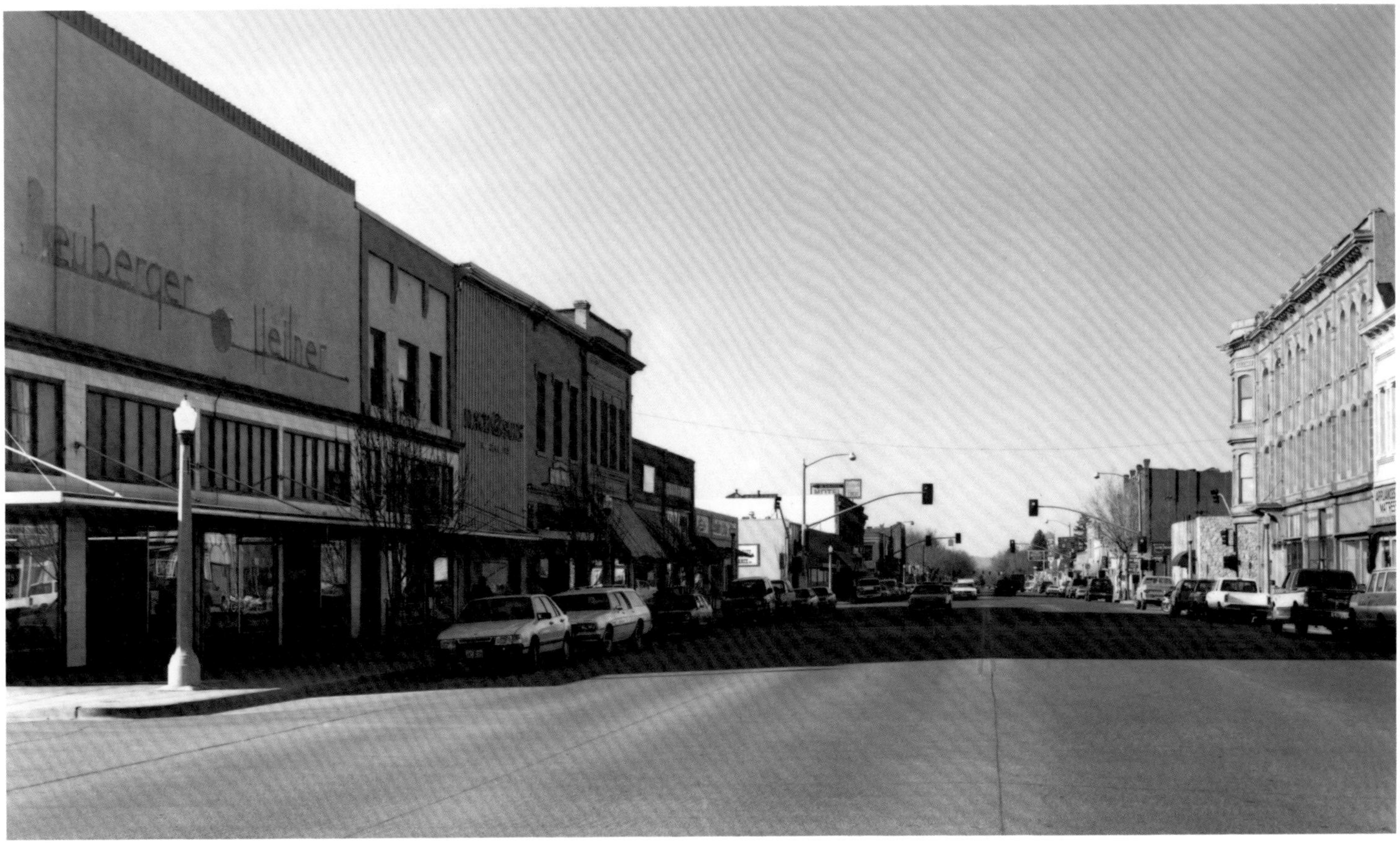

Main Street, looking north from Court, Baker City, 1994 (OHS Neg. Lot 824-34)

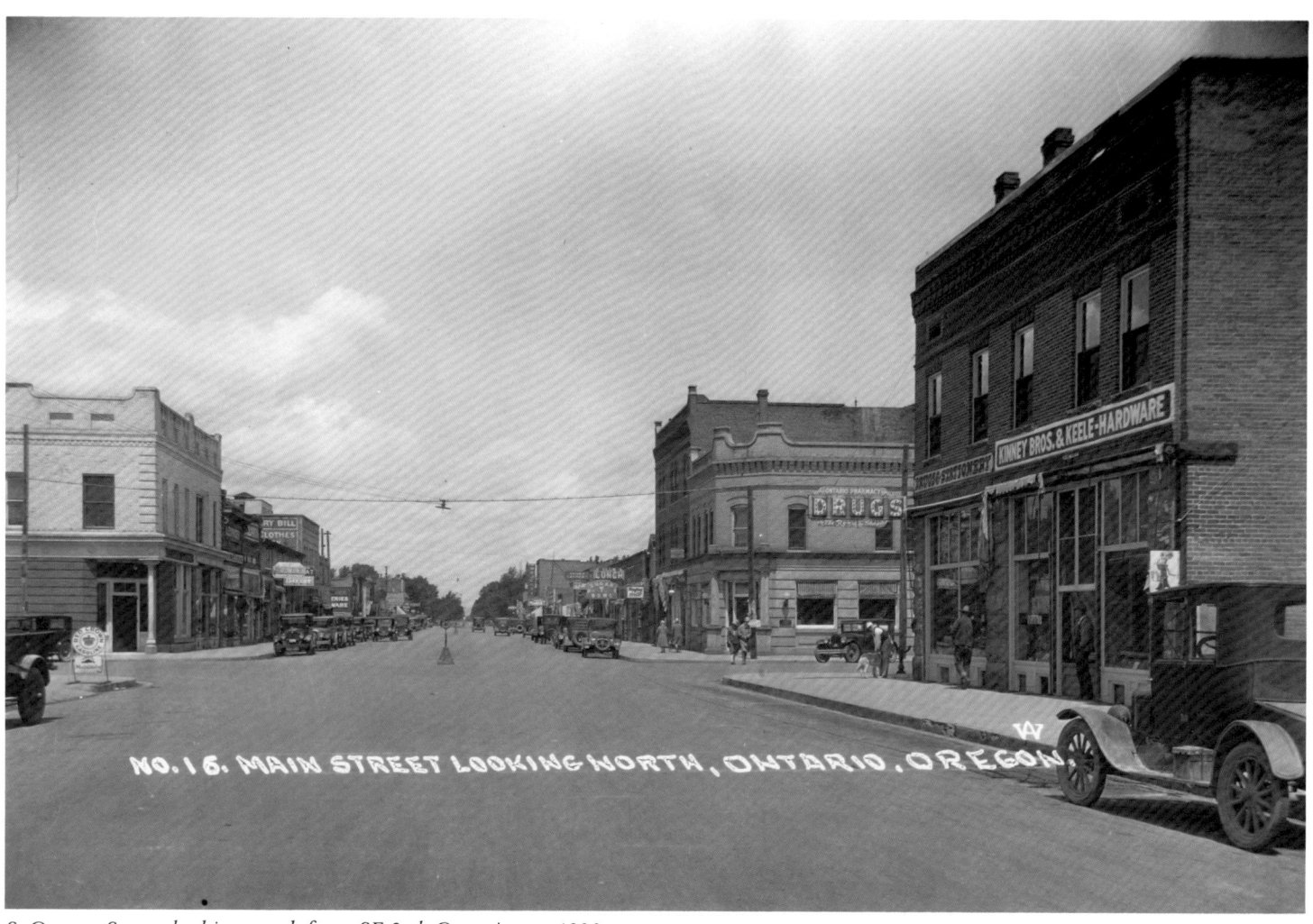

S. Oregon Street, looking north from SE 3rd, Ontario, ca. 1920 (OHS Neg. OrHi 17075)

Ontario 1920-1994

Located at the confluence of the Snake and Malheur rivers on the Idaho border, Ontario is the easternmost of Oregon's towns. Ontario's origins go back to the building of the transcontinental railroad in 1883. Four investors from Baker City filed on adjoining sections of land on the Oregon Short Line Railroad, then donated a portion of their claim to the railroad's development company in exchange for a station. One of the investors, James W. Virtue, named the station Ontario to honor his native province.

Ontario grew as a shipping point for the ranches of Harney and Malheur counties. The railroad stockyards in Ontario were extensive. Between 1884 and 1910 when the railroads reached Burns, Lakeview, and Bend, Ontario shipped much of eastern Oregon's livestock. For the pioneer ranchers, Ontario's stockyards marked the end of

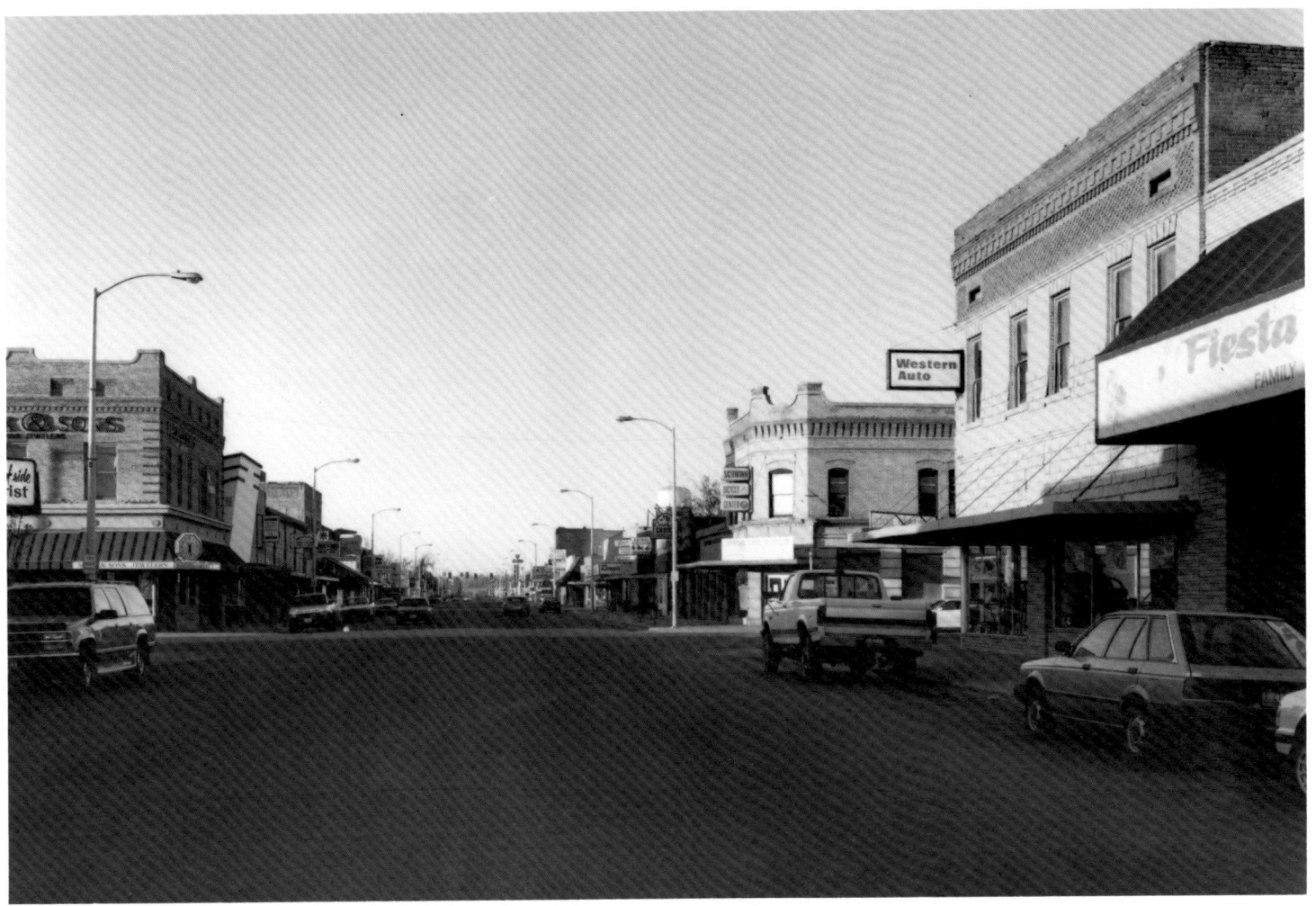

S. Oregon Street, looking north from SE 3rd, Ontario, 1994 (OHS Neg. Lot 824-35)

the long dusty drive from range to railroad. The year's calf crop would be converted to cash, and the cash exchanged for supplies to get through another year.

Most of the buildings in the historic photo were built around the turn of the century, when Ontario enjoyed its transportation monopoly. The Andrew Lackey building (1903) in the foreground housed the Ontario Pharmacy and the Kinney Brothers and Keele Hardware. The Ontario National Bank (1902) was located across the side street. Next to the bank was the three-story Carter House Hotel (1902). Across Oregon Street from the Ontario National Bank stood the First National Bank, in the James Lackey Building. Ninety years later, the scene has changed only in superficial ways. Three of the four buildings from the group remain in place. Metal awnings have replaced the canvas, and the signs and storefronts have changed. The traffic on Oregon Street is about the same, however, and the town retains much of its visual character.

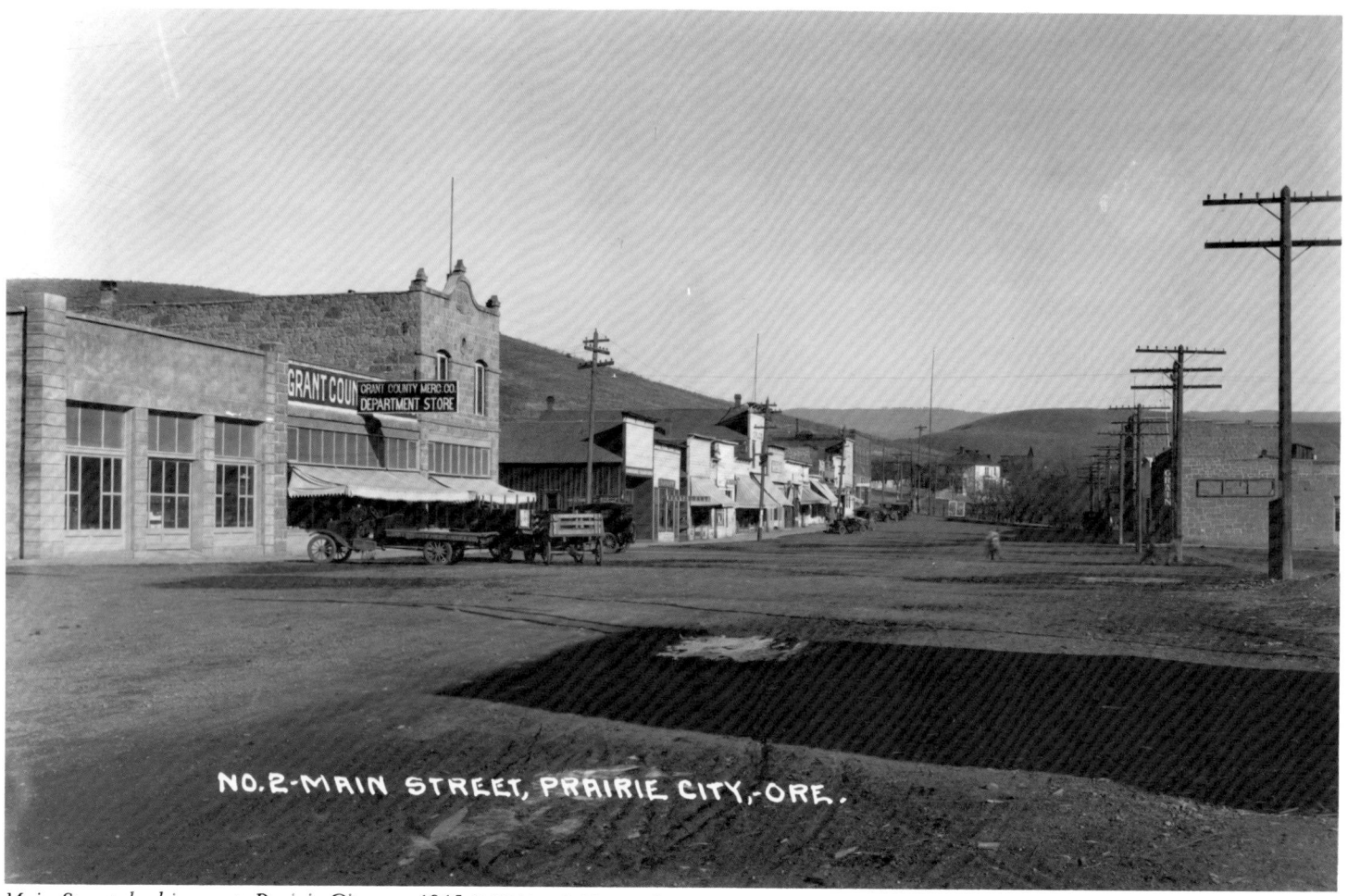

Main Street, looking east, Prairie City, ca. 1915 (OHS Neg. OrHi 17650)

Prairie City 1915-1994

Prairie City had its origin during the gold strikes of the early 1860s. The first settlement in the area was on the Dixie Creek placer claims. In 1868 the confluence of Dixie Creek and the John Day River, now the site of Prairie City, offered better opportunities for more permanent settlement. The first enterprise in town was Vinton Hartley's saloon. As placer mining waned on Dixie Creek and throughout the Blue Mountains, the new town changed from a mining camp to a commercial center for the upper John Day Valley.

At the turn of the century, Prairie City had a population of 350 permanent residents. The narrow gauge Sumpter Valley Railroad, locally called the Stump Dodger, connected Prairie City to Baker City, which lay eighty miles and three mountain

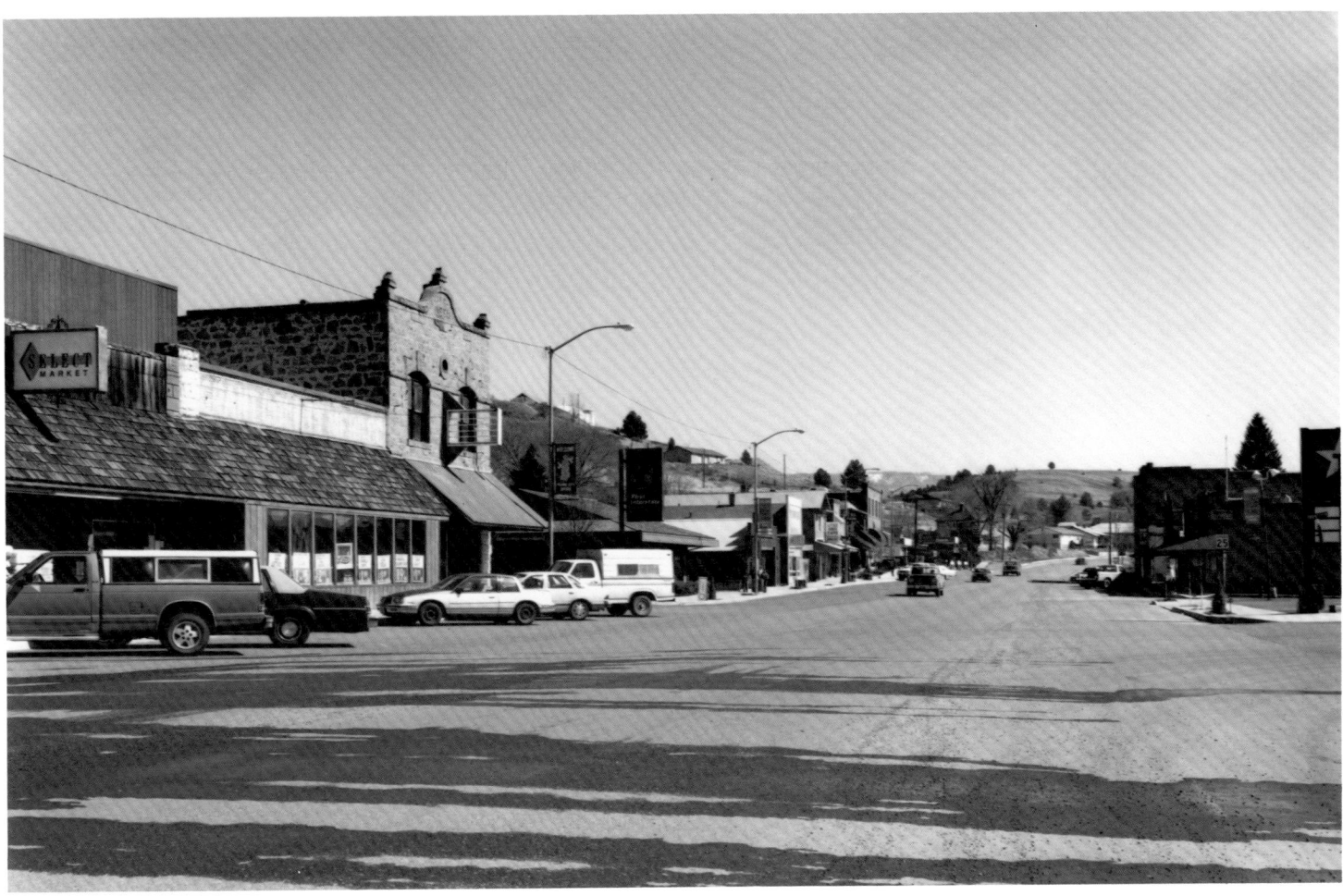

Main Street, looking east, Prairie City, 1994 (OHS Neg. Lot 824-37)

passes to the east. In addition to the stores on Main Street, Prairie City had a flour mill and a newspaper, as well as such civic amenities as schools, churches, and fraternal lodges.

The Odd Fellows Lodge and Grant County Mercantile, the stone building in the historic photo, is the descendent of one of Prairie City's first buildings, the Hyde store. The attractive light stone used for this building is volcanic tuff, a favorite material for eastern Oregon builders. Frontier masons usually built the back and sides of the buildings with random courses of uncut stone. The best material was reserved for the front of the building. Tuff was available throughout the region and offered security from the fires that periodically swept through the small towns.

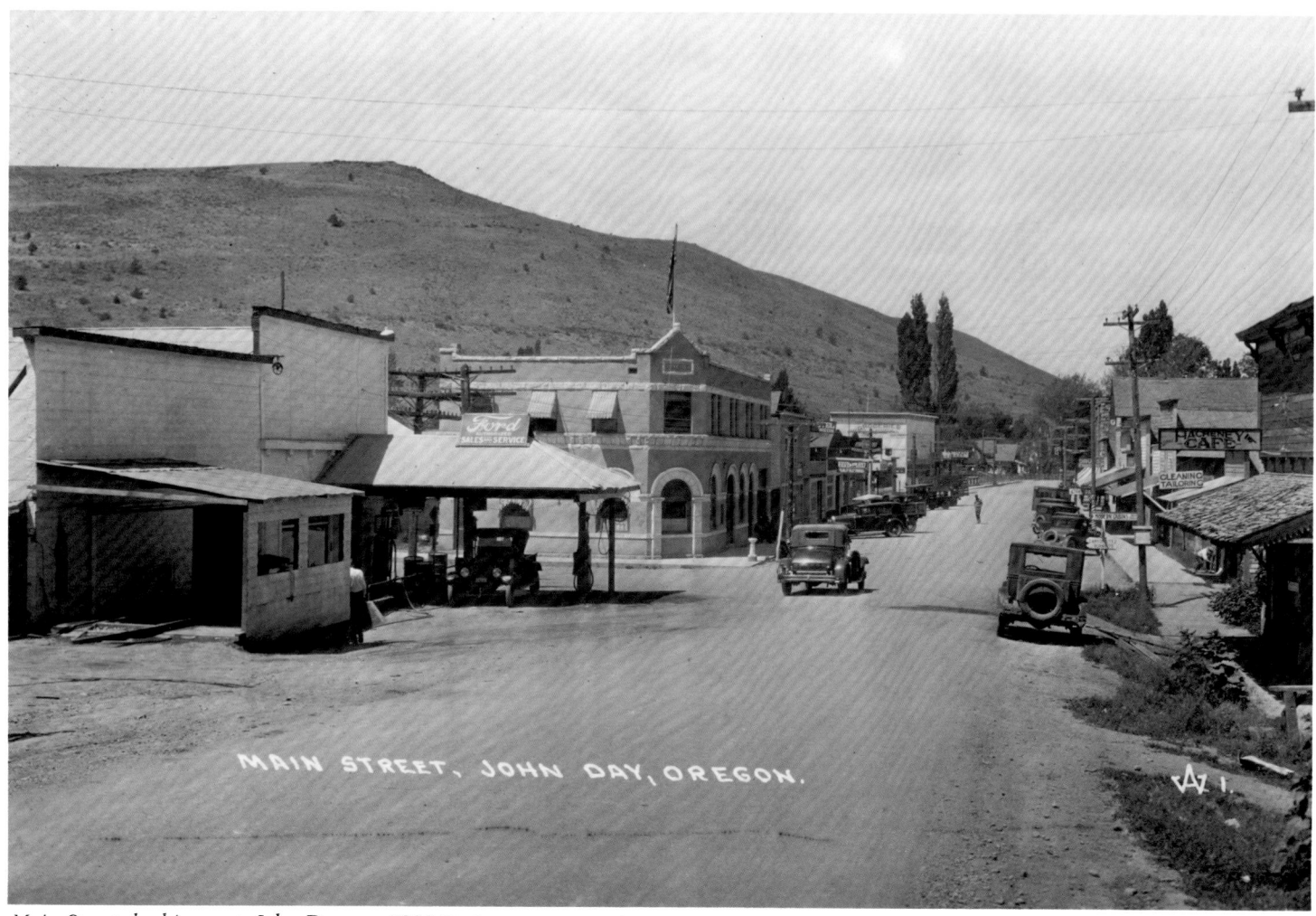

Main Street, looking east, John Day, ca. 1925 (OHS Neg. OrHi 15994)

John Day 1925-1994

Like its neighboring communities in the Blue Mountains, John Day began as a mining settlement in the early 1860s. When the Canyon Creek placers "played out" in the 1870s, gold dredging and the nearby Prairie Diggings, one of Oregon's most famous lode mines, kept the town alive. Later, ranching replaced mining in the local economy, and in more recent decades lumber mills have provided a third stage in the town's development.

In the 1890s John Day had eastern Oregon's largest Chinese community, with a population estimated by one contemporary source at 500-600 residents. As mining declined in the John Day Valley, the Chinese who remained turned to ranching, sheep

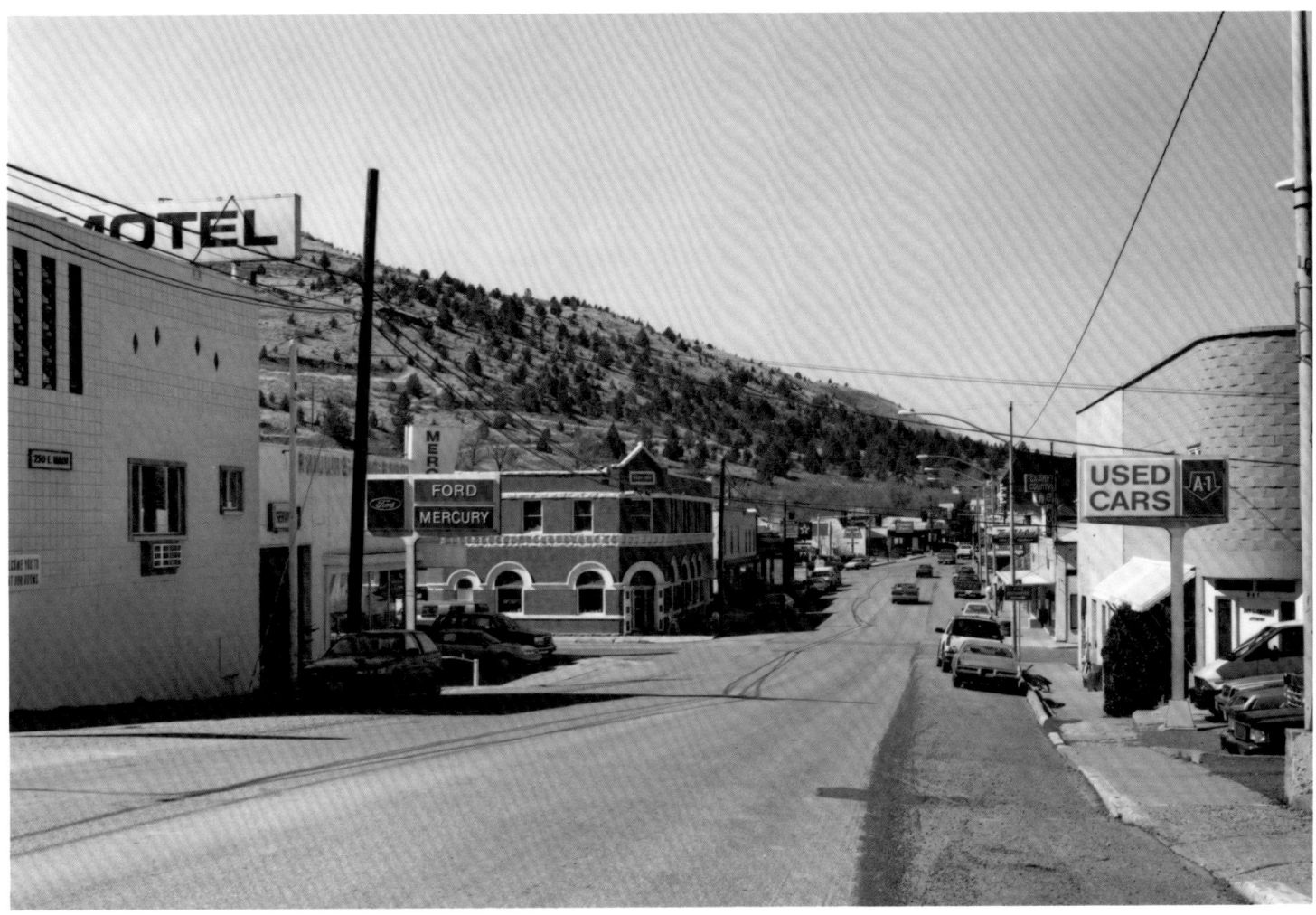

Main Street, looking east, John Day, 1994 (OHS Neg. Lot 824-38)

herding, businesses, and the professions. The Kam Wah Chung building, an early tuff structure east of Main Street, is a well-preserved reminder of the Chinese settlement.

This historic photograph shows John Day's Main street during the 1920s or early 1930s. The mixture of frame and masonry buildings is unusual in a town of this size, where we might expect to see a higher percentage of brick or stone buildings. One reason that frame buildings survived on Main Street is that John Day managed to escape the fires that leveled most eastern Oregon towns in the 1880s or 1890s.

Bend 1920-1994

A late arrival among the communities east of the Cascades, Bend was platted at the turn of the century by Alexander Drake, a fast-talking promoter from Minneapolis. Bend boomed as people from the Midwest poured in to file claims on the "free Government timber" that surrounded the town. Dr. Urling Coe, Bend's first physician, described a street scene in 1905: "Freighters, stockmen, buckaroos, sheep herders, timber cruisers, gamblers, and transients of all kinds...thronged the bars or played at the gambling games."

Despite its rowdy start, Bend stabilized in the first decade of the century. Irrigation canals watered the desert and the Deschutes Valley begin to attract settlers. Novelist H. L. Davis strolled down Bend's Wall Street, listening to the languages of Basque stockmen, Norwegian loggers, Mexican *vaqueros*, and Irish sheep-herders. In 1911 the railroad came to town, and in its wake came the lumber mills that transformed Bend from a boom town to a mill town.

The photo of Bond Street, taken perhaps in the early 1920s, shows automobiles, street lights, and masonry buildings--hallmarks of a thriving community. The surprisingly modern O'Kane Building, the light-colored structure on the west side of the street, was built in 1915. Its owner, Hugh O'Kane, was an innkeeper, entrepreneur, fight-promoter, gambler, raconteur, and all-around Bend character. Now fully restored to National Register standards, the O'Kane Building houses restaurants, businesses, and offices--the civilized blend of services and tourism that points the way to Bend's future.

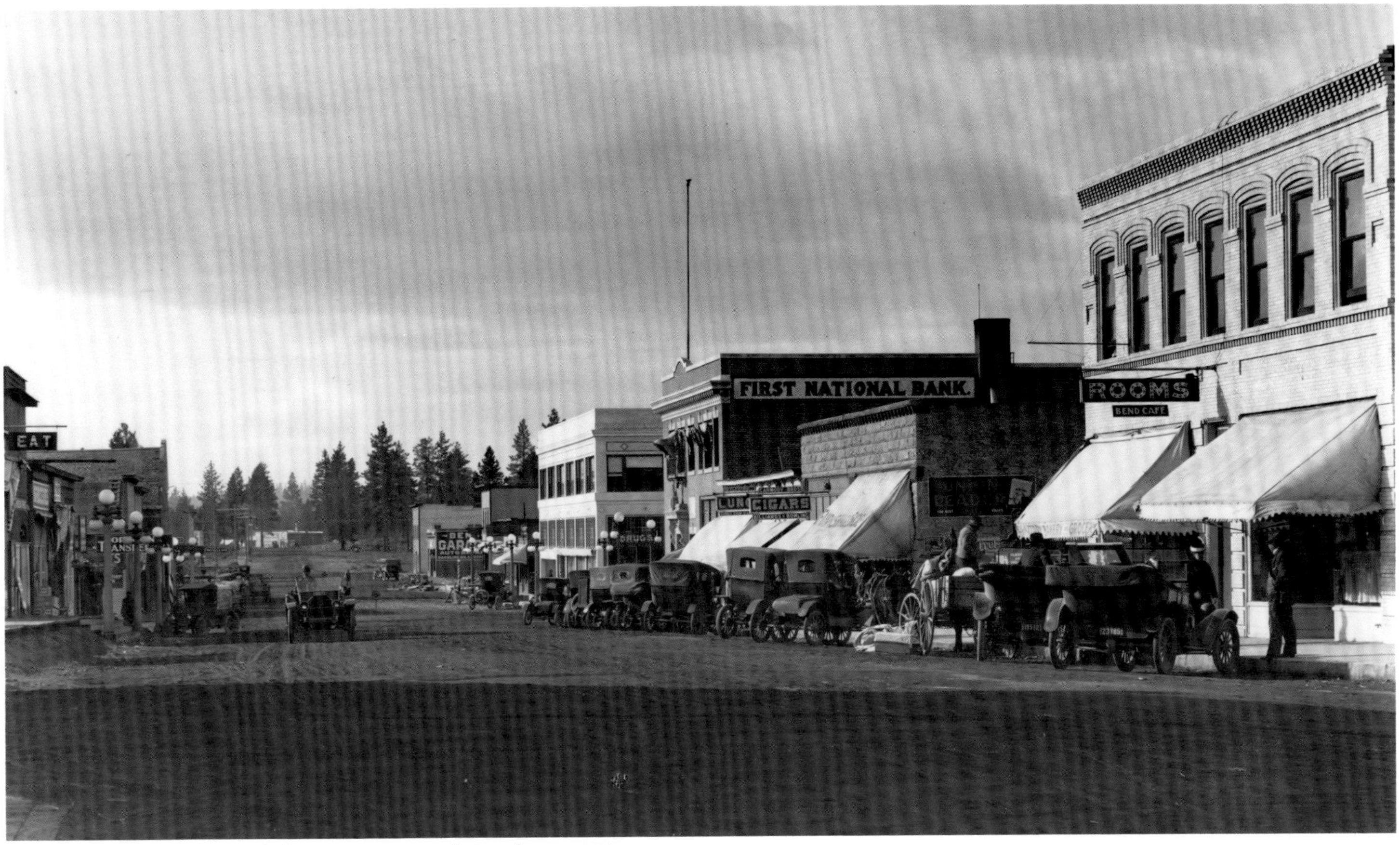

Bond Street, looking south from Greenwood, Bend, ca. 1920 (OHS Neg. OrHi Gi6836)

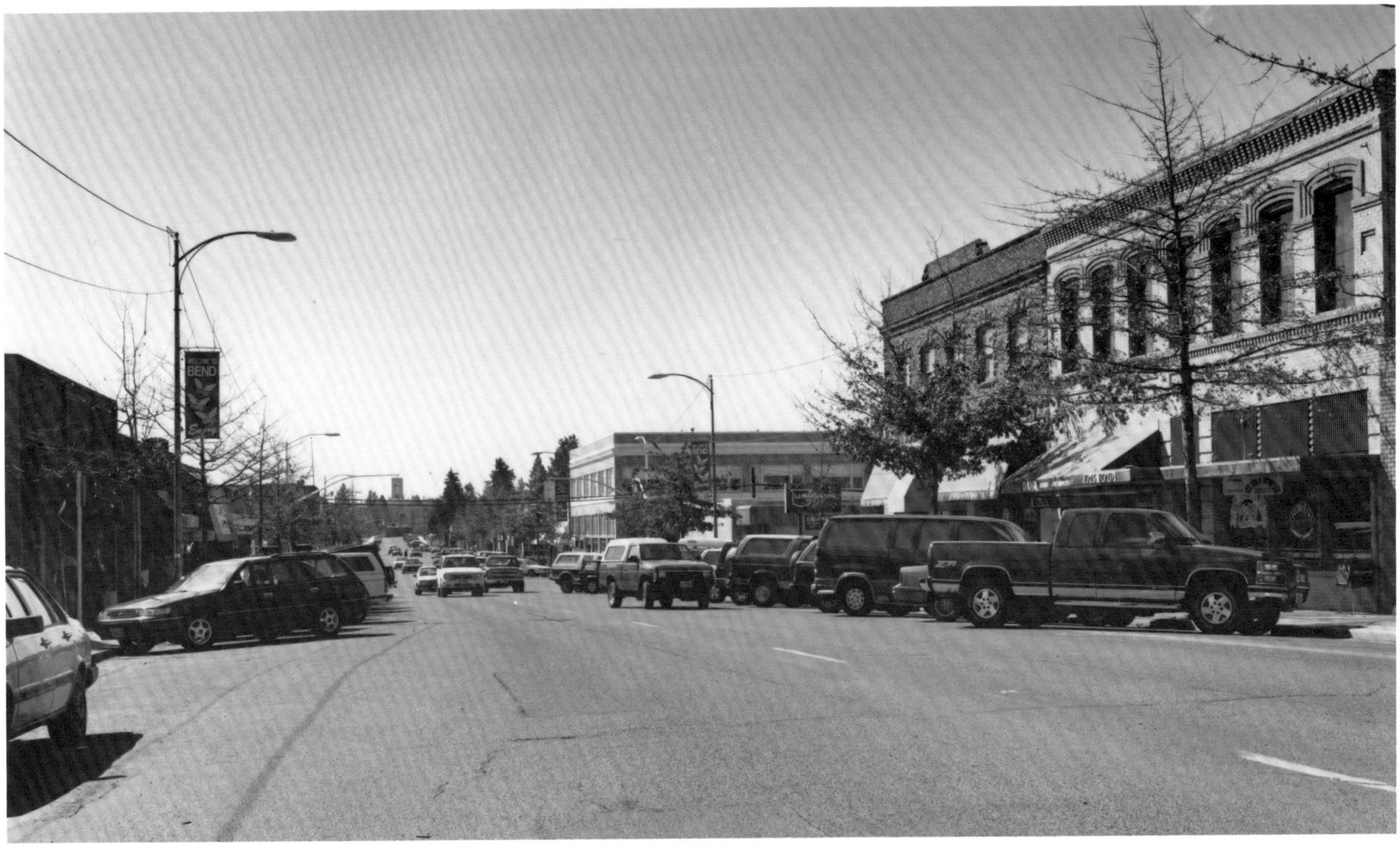

Bond Street, looking south from Greenwood, Bend, 1994 (OHS Neg. Lot 824-39)

Klamath Falls 1915-1994

Klamath Falls began as Linkville in the 1870s, a settlement of Euro-Americans on Link River between Upper Klamath Lake and Lake Ewauna. The town grew slowly through the 1880s and 1890s as a modest trading center for the farms and ranches of the Klamath Basin and for the Klamath Reservation to the north.

Then, soon after the turn of the century, the pace of life began to quicken. Irrigation canals brought water from Upper Klamath Lake to the rich bottom lands of southern Klamath County. The Southern Pacific built a railroad north from California. By 1920, Klamath County had twenty-four saw mills; by the end of the decade, the Basin was producing 3,000,000 board feet of pine each working day. For a few heady years in the late 1920s, Klamath Falls was Oregon's third largest city, with a population greater than Eugene's.

The building in the foreground of the historic photo is the Wintherow-Melhase Block, which housed the Stevens Hotel. Brick and masonry commercial buildings like the Stevens Hotel are a feature of most towns east of the Cascades. Built in 1906, the building had suffered various indignities over the years, but had been renovated recently and was listed on the National Register. Unfortunately, it was seriously damaged by an earthquake on September 20, 1993. In March of 1994, the building was razed and a new structure was started on the site.

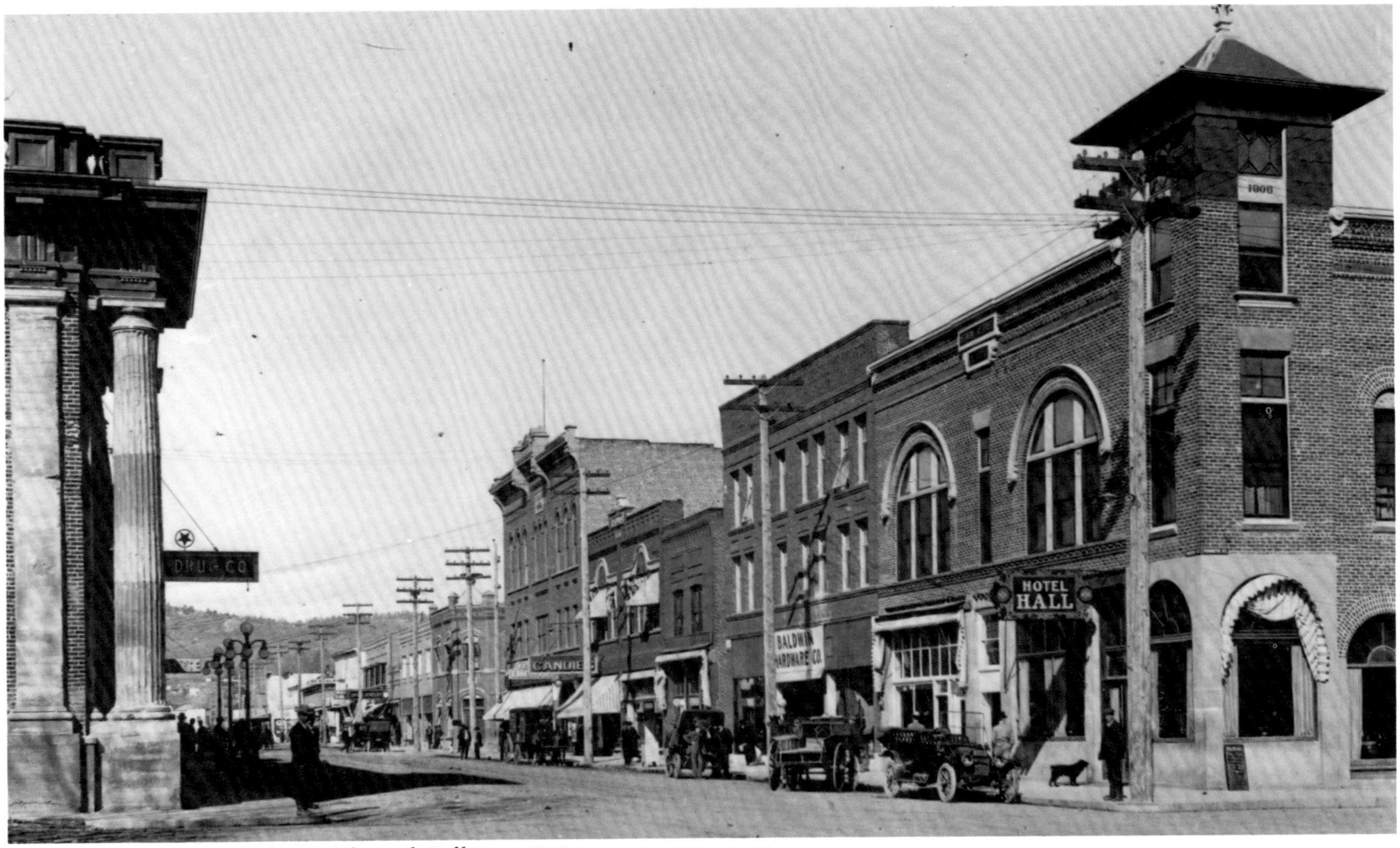

Main Street, looking northeast, Klamath Falls, ca. 1915 (OHS Neg. CN 010479)

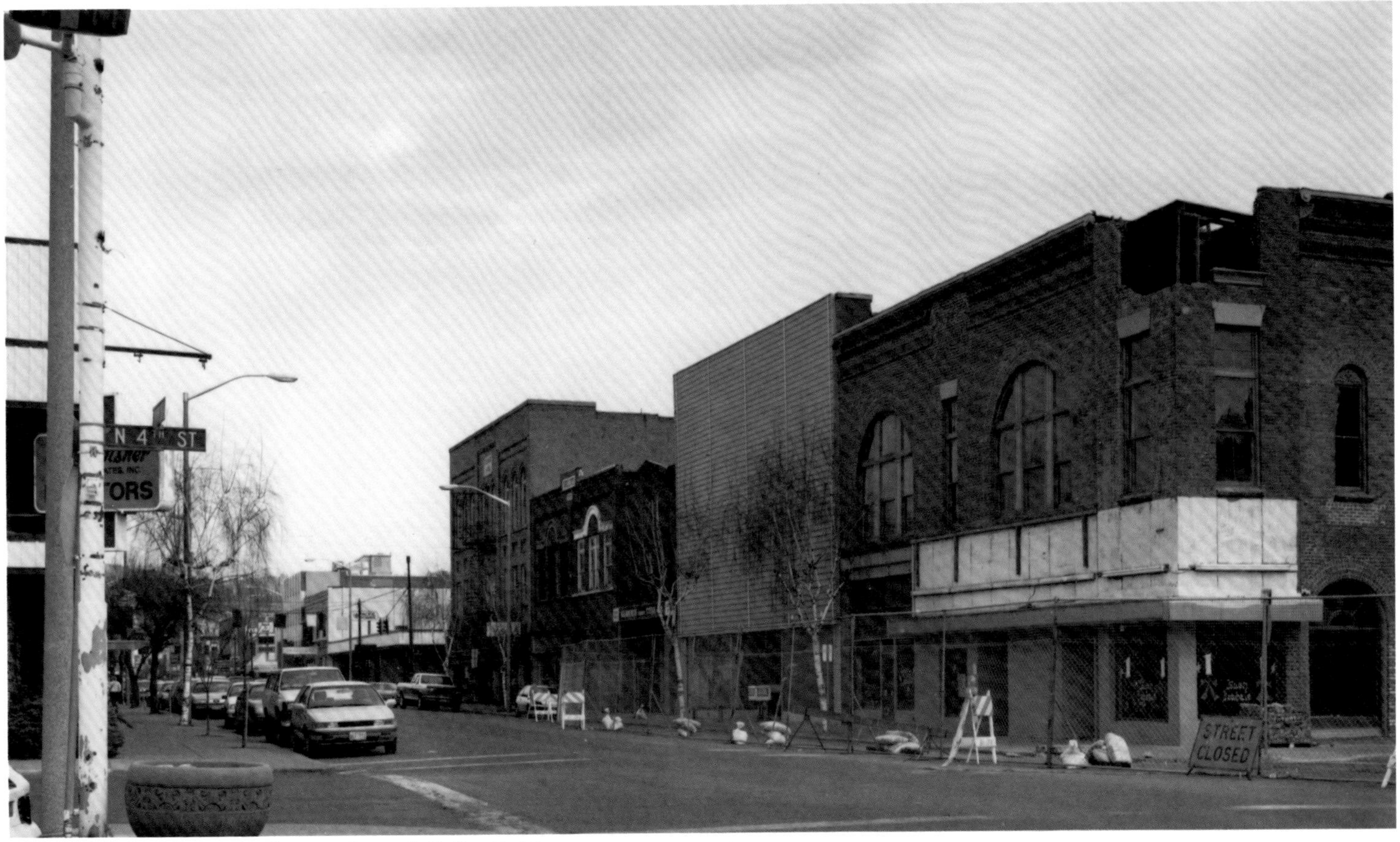

Main Street, looking northeast, Klamath Falls, 1994 (OHS Neg. Lot 824-42)

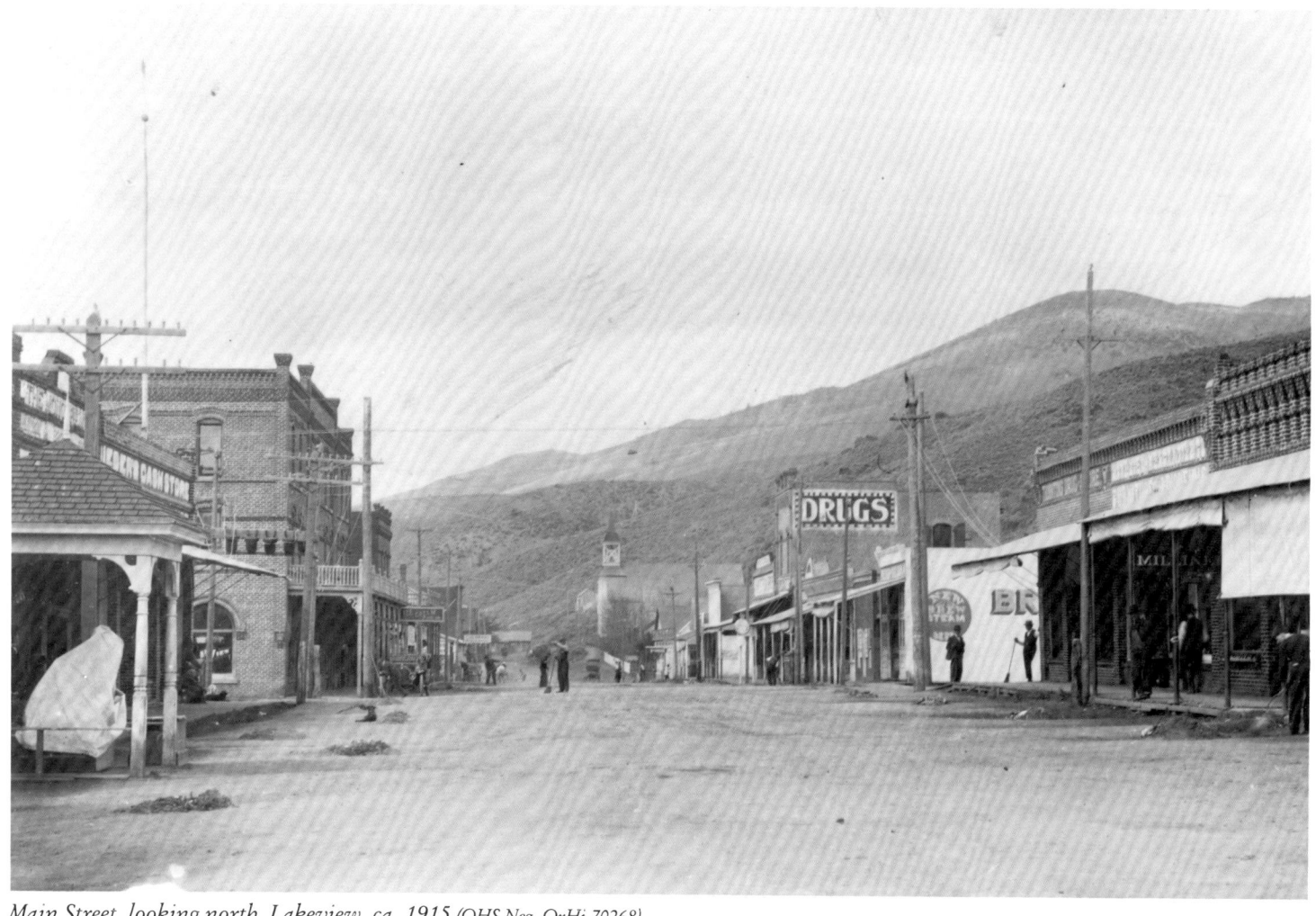

Main Street, looking north, Lakeview, ca. 1915 (OHS Neg. OrHi 70268)

Lakeview 1915-1994

While other towns east of the Cascades started with gold rushes or timber booms, Lakeview was founded for political expediency. In 1874 the only town in Lake County was Linkville, located on Klamath Lake and inconvenient to the settlers in the Goose Lake Valley. The Goose Lake people started Lakeview so that they could move the county seat to their own neighborhood.

Lakeview developed in the 1870s and 1880s as a commercial center for the ranches of south central Oregon. Sheep ranching flourished, and Lakeview became a favorite destination for immigrants from the west counties of Ireland. In one old story, a sheep-herder from County Cork sends his nephew passage money and some advice: "Mikey, my boy, come straight to Lakeview. Don't bother stopping in America at all."

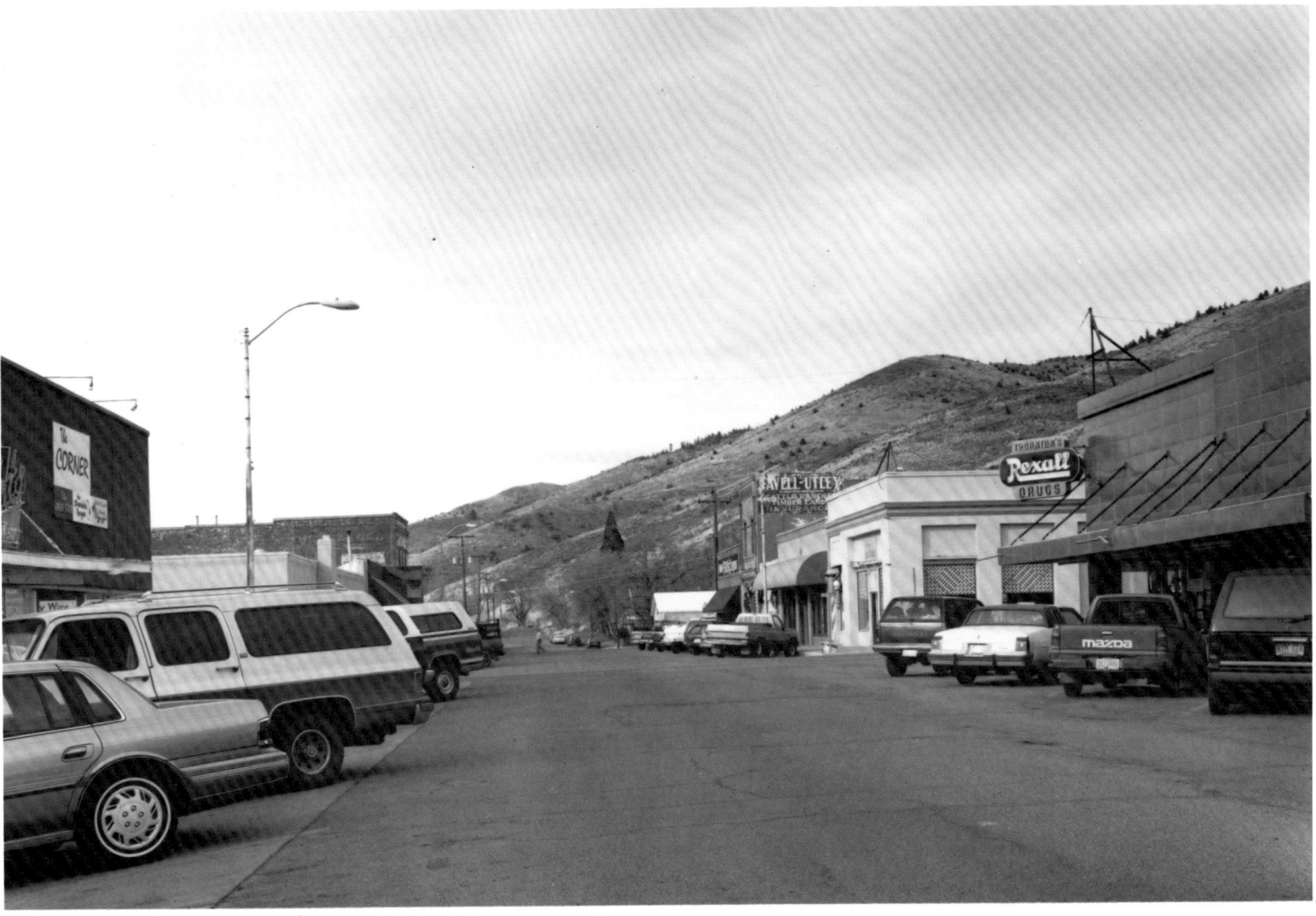

Main Street, looking north, Lakeview, 1994 (OHS Neg. Lot 824-43)

The historic scene on "E" Street shows men sweeping the street in a leisurely fashion. Traffic is not a problem. On the right side of the street is the two-story Bank of Lakeview building, now Favell-Utley. This brick structure was built in 1889 and is one of the few downtown buildings to survive the disastrous fire of May 22, 1900. Across the street is the Post and King building, site of the Kentucky Saloon. This building went up soon after the fire, during the summer of 1900. The Kentucky Saloon and its clientele were a feature of Lakeview's Main street from the turn of the century until Prohibition.

BIBLIOGRAPHY

Alinder, James (ed.) *Carleton E. Watkins: Photographs of the Columbia River and Oregon.* Friends of Photography, Inc., and Weston Gallery, Santa Barbara. 1979.

Atwood, Kay. *Medford, Oregon: Historic Context.* City of Medford, Oregon, 1993.

Bailey, Ruth. *Main Street, Northeast Oregon.* Oregon Historical Society Press, Portland, 1982.

Brogan, Phil. *East of the Cascades.* Binford and Mort, Portland, 1971.

Carey, Charles H. *General History of Oregon.* Binfords and Mort, Portland, 1971.

Corning, Howard M. (ed). *Dictionary of Oregon History.* Binford and Mort Publishing, Portland, 1989.

_____. *Willamette Landings: Ghost Towns of the River.* Second Edition, Oregon Historical Society Press, Portland, 1973.

Culp, Edwin D. *Oregon, The Way It Was.* Caxton Printers, Caldwell, 1989.

Dicken, Samuel N. and Emily F., *The Making of Oregon.* Oregon Historical Society, Portland, 1979.

Dodge, Orvil. *Pioneer History of Coos and Curry Counties, Oregon.* Capitol Printing Co., Salem, 1898. (Second Edition, with errata, Coos-Curry Pioneer and Historical Society, 1969.)

Douthit, Nathan. *A Guide to Oregon South Coast History.* River West Books, Coos Bay, 1986.

Dutton, A. A. *Arizona: Then and Now.* Ag2 Press, Phoenix, 1981.

Evans, Gail E. H. *Jacksonville Historical Survey.* City of Jacksonville, Oregon, 1980.

Gaston, Joseph. *The Centennial History of Oregon.* S.J. Clarke Publishing Company, Portland, 1912.

Gernsheim, Helmut. *The Origins of Photography.* Thames and Hudson, New York, 1982.

Gottfried and Jennings. *American Vernacular Design: 1870-1940.* Iowa State University Press, Ames, 1988.

Gregg, J. R. *Pioneer Days in Malheur County.* Private Print by L. L. Morrison, Los Angeles, 1950.

Goin, Peter. *Stopping Time: A Rephotographic Survey of Lake Tahoe.* University of New Mexico Press, Albuquerque, 1992.

Good, Rachael Applegate. *A History of Klamath County, Oregon.* Klamath Falls, 1941.

Hales, Peter Bacon. *Silver Cities: The Photography of American Urbanization, 1839-1915.* Temple University Press, Philadelphia, 1984.

[Harbour, Terry.] *Cultural and Historic Resources Inventory of Myrtle Creek, Oregon.* City of Myrtle Creek, Oregon, 1984.

Holtgrieve, Donald G. *Historical Geography of Transportation Routes and Town Populations in Oregon's Willamette Valley.* Unpublished Doctoral Dissertation, Department of Geography, University of Oregon, Eugene, 1973.

An Illustrated History of Baker, Grant, Malheur, and Harney Counties. Western Historical Publishing Co., Spokane, 1902.

An Illustrated History of Union and Wallowa Counties. Western Historical Publishing Co., Spokane, 1902.

Kadas, Marianne. *Roseburg Business District Historic Context and Cultural Resources Inventory.* City of Roseburg, Oregon, 1991.

Keisling, Phil, Secretary of State. *1993-94 Oregon Blue Book.* Oregon State Printing Office, Salem, 1993.

Klett, Mark and Manchester, Ellen and Verburg, JoAnn. *Second View: The Rephotographic Survey Project.* University of New Mexico Press, Albuquerque, 1984.

Koler/Morrison Planning Consultants. *City of Coquille Historic Resource Inventory.* City of Coquille, Oregon, 1988.

Kramer, George. *Survey of Historic and Cultural Resources: Downtown Commercial Area, Phase 1.* City of Medford, Oregon, 1994.

_____. *1993 Historic and Cultural Resource Inventory; A Historic Context Statement for the City of Jacksonville, Oregon.* City of Jacksonville, Oregon, 1993.

Kramer, George and Chappel, Jill Anne. *Historic Resources Survey and Inventory of the Central Business District.* City of Grants Pass, Oregon, 1992.

Lockley, Fred. *History of the Columbia River Valley From the Dalles to the Sea, Vol.I.* S.J. Clark, Chicago, 1928. _

Loy, William G. Stuart Allan, Clyde P. Patton, and Robert D. Plank. *Atlas of Oregon.* University of Oregon Books, Eugene, 1976.

Marker, Sherry. *America: Then and Now.* Barnes and Nobles, Inc., New York and Brompton Books, Greenwich, 1993.

McArthur, Lewis A. *Oregon Geographic Names.* Sixth Edition, revised by Lewis L. McArthur, Oregon Historical Society Press, Portland, 1992.

Mumford, Lewis. *The City in History: Its Origins, Its Transformations, and Its Prospects.* Harcourt, Brace and World, Inc., New York, 1961.

Naef, Weston J., and Wood, James N. *Era of Exploration.* New York Graphic Society, Boston, 1975.

O'Harra, Marjorie Lutz. *Ashland: The First 130 Years.* Revised edition, Northwest Passages Publishing, Ashland, 1986.

Pare, Richard. *Photography and Architecture: 1839-1939.* MIT Press, Cambridge, 1985.

Parsons, William and Shiack, W. S. *A History of Umatilla County and A History of Morrow County.* W. H. Lever, Spokane, 1902.

Peterson, Emil R. and Powers, Alfred. *A Century of Coos and Curry.* Binfords and Mort, Portland, 1952.

Preston, R. N. *Maps of Historical Oregon.* Western Guide Publishers, Corvallis, 1972.

Price, Nancy Waterman. "The Coos Bay Hotel Company and the Building of the Chandler Hotel." *Coos Historical Journal*, Autumn, 1985.

The Progress Number. Coquille Valley Sentinel, June 1937.

Robinson, Cervin and Herschman, Joel. *Architecture Transformed: A History of the Photography of Buildings from 1839 to the Present.* MIT Press, Cambridge, 1987.

Robinson, Tom. *Oregon Photographers: Biographical History and Directory, 1852-1917.* 2nd Edition, Portland, 1993.

Sandweiss, Martha A. (ed.) *Photography in Nineteenth-Century America.* Amon Carter Museum, Fort Worth and Harry N. Abrams, Inc., Publishers, New York, 1991.

Seiberling, Grace with Carolyn Bloore. *Amateurs, Photography, and the Mid-Victorian Imagination.* University of Chicago Press, Chicago, 1986.

Stamp, Gavin. *The Changing Metropolis.* Penguin Books, New York, 1986.

Szarkowski, John. *Photography Until Now.* Museum of Modern Art, New York, 1989.

Toedtemeier, Terry. "Oregon Photography: The First Fifty Years." *Oregon Historical Quarterly*, Spring 1993.

Vaughan, Thomas, and Ferriday, Virginia. *Space, Style, and Structure.* Oregon Historical Society, Portland, 1974.

Walling, A. G. *History of Southern Oregon.* A. G. Walling, Portland, 1884.

Yenne, Bill (ed.) *The Opening of the American West in Early Photographs and Prints.* Chartwell Books, New Jersey, 1993.

INDEX

Technical Notes

The contemporary photographs were made using a tripod-mounted Cambo monorail-type 4x5" view camera. All of the images were made with either a Rodenstock 135mm f/5.6 lens or a Nikkor SW 90mm f/8 lens. For long-term storage, all photographic materials were prepared on archivally-processed Kodak T-MAX 100 black and white film, and reposited in the collection of the Oregon Historical Society.

To accommodate the architectural nature of the subject matter and to match the historic views, each image was perspective controlled. While much care was taken to determine the exact original position from which the historic photo was made, it was not always feasible to rephotograph the scene from that location. Often, traffic signal standards, signage, or even trees, planted to "re-pedestrianize" main street obscured the view as it was originally recorded, and forced a slight modification of positioning for the rephotograph.

About the Authors

James Norman, photographer and project director for Oregon Main Street, is a cultural historian with the Oregon Department of Transportation. Mr. Norman's previous publications include *Portland's Architectural Heritage* (OHS Press, 1991), *Historic Highway Bridges of Oregon* (OHS Press, 1989), and *Oregon Covered Bridges: A Study for the 1989-90 Legislature* (ODOT, 1989). His documentary and fine arts photography has also been published in such books as *American Landscape Architecture* (Preservation Press, 1989) and *The Best of Photography Annual: 1985* (Photographers Forum, 1985), exhibited in galleries and museums ranging from Kawagoe, Japan to Washington, D.C., and included in the permanent collections of the Seattle Art Museum, the Portland Art Museum, the National Trust for Historic Preservation, the National Register of Historic Places, the Smithsonian Institution, the Library of Congress, and the Oregon Historical Society.

Rosalind Clark Keeney is a Cultural Historian with the Oregon Department of Transportation, and a Preservation Planner for the City of Albany. She is also the author of *Architecture, Oregon Style* (Professional Book Center, 1983), one of the most widely used research references regarding the history and development of architecture in Oregon. Mrs. Keeney currently serves on the Albany and Linn County Landmarks Commissions, and was the recipient of a Historic Preservation award from the Historic Preservation League of Oregon in 1980.

George Kramer is a noted consultant in the field of historic preservation. He serves on the Board of Directors for the Historic Preservation League of Oregon and the Siskiyou Pioneer Sites Foundation, and was presented the "Preservationist of the Year" award in 1992 by the City of Ashland, Oregon Historic Commission. Mr. Kramer is the author of several articles regarding Oregon's cultural history, and his master's thesis examined the impact of regulation on the historic commercial landscape in Oregon.

Dwight A. Smith is a Senior Cultural Historian with the Oregon Department of Transportation. Mr. Smith was the principal author of *Historic Highway Bridges of Oregon* (OHS Press), and prepared the National Register nomination for the Historic Columbia River Highway. He has served on numerous historic preservation organizations, including the National Transportation Research Board Committee on Historic Preservation and Archaeology, and is currently a member of the State Legislative Task Force on Oregon's Heritage

Dr. Ward Tonsfeldt, Professor of Humanities at Central Oregon Community College, is widely regarded as one of Oregon's most prominent humanities scholars. Dr. Tonsfeldt currently serves as Vice-Chair for both the State Advisory Committee for Historic Preservation and the Deschutes County Landmarks Commission, and has participated in several recent NEH and OCH-sponsored projects. He has authored numerous articles, cultural resource surveys, and regional studies regarding Oregon's cultural history.

Colophon

The text stock for Oregon Main Street is 100# Matrix Dull offset. The photographic images have been printed as spot-varnished 200-line duotones prepared by Your Town Press, Salem, Oregon. The typeface for the text is Garamond. For durability, the bindings for both the hard and soft cover editions are Smythe-sewn.

Oregon Main Street was designed by James B. Norman Jr.